CAROLINE FRANCZIA

POPCORN
FOR THE NEW
CEO

Snackable content & Business insights out of 300 office hours with C-Level executives from B2B European startups and scaleups.

'Here's to the crazy ones, the misfits, the rebels, the troublemakers, the round pegs in the square holes ... the ones who see things differently.

They're not fond of rules, and they have no respect for the status quo.

You can quote them, disagree with them, glorify or vilify them, but the only thing you can't do is ignore them because they change things.

They push the human race forward, and while some may see them as the crazy ones, we see genius, because the people who are crazy enough to think that they can change the world, are the ones who do.'

Steve Jobs

DEDICATION

To Romeo, your imagination is exhilarating, your curiosity for knowledge challenges us to be better every day.

To Theodore, you are the example of drive and resilience, your strength is contagious.

FOREWORD	5
INTRODUCTION	6
BOOK I: PLANT THE SEED	7
CHAP 1: MINDSET BOOST	8
CHAP 2: CREATE & ITERATE YOUR VALUE PROPOSITION	14
CHAP 3: STOP PITCHING, EVEN IF YOU'RE CEO	20
CHAP 4: ENTREPRENEURS & ADAPTABILITY QUOTIENT	27
CHAP 5: NO BULLYING & SAFE CULTURE	31
CHAP 6: SEGMENT & CHOOSE YOUR FIRST CUSTOMERS	38
CHAP 7: PROSPECTING MASTERPLAN	43
BOOK II: BUILD IT UP	51
CHAP 8: AVOID THE BURN OUT	52
CHAP 9: THE QUESTION OF GOING FREEMIUM	59
CHAP 10: POC vs PILOT EXPLAINED	65
CHAP 11: NO CHAMPION, NO DEAL	72
CHAP 12: PRICING STRATEGY & MARGIN	78
CHAP 13: NEGOTIATIONS SKILLS	86
CHAP 14: SALES FORECAST ACCURACY	91
CHAP 15: THE DATA DRIVEN COMPANY	99
CHAP 16: EACH TEAM IMPACTS THE REVENUE	108
CHAP 17: MEDDIC AS A COMMON LANGUAGE	114
CHAP 18: 0% CHURN OBJECTIVE	124
BOOK III: SCALE IT UP	131
CHAP 19: THE SDR VALUE	132
CHAP 20: SALES PROCESS IN THE SUBSCRIPTION ERA	137
CHAP 21: TARGET AND ACHIEVE COMPLEX DEALS	145
CHAP 22: FIGHT THE COMPETITION	151
CHAP 23: THE ART OF THE COMPENSATION PLAN	158
CHAP 24: HUNT & HIRE TOP TALENT	164
CHAP 25: TOP ACHIEVER MANAGEMENT	170
CHAP 26: PROMOTE OR NOT PROMOTE	175
CHAP 27: OBJECTIONS AND REJECTIONS	183
UNTIL THE SEQUEL	191
THANK YOU SPEECH	192
ABOUT THE AUTHOR	195

FOREWORD

'Popcorn for the New CEO is a witty and wise must-read for entrepreneurs and business owners. Full of relatable quotes, well-crafted tips, and quick case studies, this book is the Millennium Falcon you've been waiting for to take you and your company to the new heights of business success.' – *Ekaterina Walter, Wall Street Journal bestselling author.*[1]

'Each chapter reflects on what we went through during our own startup journey. The book offers the right business shortcuts distilled with Hollywood Blockbusters. At Logomatic.io, we often went the wrong way and figured it out from there. I wish we received lessons from a Jedi master at the time. In retrospect, it makes sense not to push a product just because you have it.' – *Amirhossein Malekzadeh, Co-founder and CEO of Logmatic.io acquired by Datadog.Inc.*

---

[1]'The Laws of Brand Storytelling: Win – and Keep – Your Customers' Hearts and Minds'
'Think Like Zuck: The Five Business Secrets of Facebook's Improbably Brilliant CEO Mark Zuckerberg'
'The Power of Visual Storytelling: How to Use Visuals, Videos, and Social Media to Market Your Brand'

INTRODUCTION

This book was during the year of 2020, a challenging time for all of us. Nevertheless, with burdensome times rise opportunities, and for me, it was to create Uppercut-First.

In thematic chapters, this manuscript compiles the brainstorming sessions held during office hours with Seed to Serie B European CEOs and their executive teams.

It is with actionable insights in mind that I created a book that you can read as you need, to support your experiences on the field. You may read it all at once or…

Read the chapter that may be the best answer to what is bothering you right now.

BOOK I

PLANT THE SEED

CHAP 1: MINDSET BOOST

The wolf of wall street

Success in the startup world requires vision and agility, drive, commitment, and the capacity to let go. No excuses, no whining, no arguing. Something that is commonly referred to as: The Mindset. A quality that Jordan Belfort has made quite popular in his autobiographical movie: The Wolf of Wall street

When it comes to success, the Mindset is an incredible element that a lot of people miss. It is the difference between the hard worker that slowly progresses to a managerial level position and the self-made billionaire.

--The product--

Jordan Belfort: 'The easiest way to make money is -create something of such value that everybody wants and go out and give and create value, the money comes automatically.'

This seems simple enough, although I keep meeting people who create a product and only then, try to associate some kind of value. The notion of unique differentiators (also known as USPs for Unique Selling Proposition) should come to your mind when you define the vision of your company. How will you continue systematically to differentiate yourself in ways that no one else can? If you do not have that on the tip of your tongue as you read this, run to your R&D people and ask them.

--The delivery--

Jordan Belfort: 'Without action, the best intentions in the world are nothing more than that: intentions.'

You've made promises to your investors about the forecast, to your customers about the roadmap, to your team about hiring, yet you're overwhelmed, you can't seem to delegate, and soon enough, your best intentions remain what they are: best intentions. Make a plan, associate deadlines, track the delivery.

As a CEO, you are not supposed to manage the sales forecast, yet you must rely upon your sales team reporting accuracy when attending your board meeting.

As a CEO, you are not supposed to manage the roadmap and deliveries, yet, if customers churn and others don't sign, it will impact your company in ways you did not predict.

-The sales—

Jordan Belford: 'Act as if you have unmatched confidence, and then people will surely have confidence in you. Act as if you have an unmatched experience, and then people will follow your advice. And act as if you are already a tremendous success, and as sure as I stand here today – you will become successful.'

When it comes to sales, 80% of the job is to find the right people with the right soft skills. People that have drive and confidence, some experience but remain highly coachable, the ones who learn fast but never stop learning. The one who truly wants to make a difference and stand out by effectively hunting while remaining a trusted advisor.

The key is for the person in the role of the salesperson to 'act as if':

- ☐ You already have a hundred customers even if you only have ten
- ☐ To believe he/she can sell at an Annual Contract Value of 400K even though your average size deal is 80K
- ☐ To create audacious proposals even though they've just joined the company.

--No success without failure—

Jordan Belfort: 'People tend to give up. If you have persistence, you will come out ahead of most people. More importantly, you will learn. When you do something, you might fail. But that's not because you're a failure. It's because you have not learned enough. Do it differently each time. One day, you will do it right. Failure is your friend.'

It is OK to fail. Repeat after me. Repetition is essential because, from a collective point of view, we remain, on this side of the pond -meaning in Europe- quite afraid of failure. And that's because we've missed the point. Failing is a way to learn and grow. Who in the world has started walking without ever falling?

Those who failed fast and learned from it are the most impressive example of success. If you haven't yet, check out the stories of Theodor Seuss Geisel, Oprah Winfrey, J.K Rowling, Thomas Edison, Steve Jobs, and more.

As a successful CEO, you should always aim for success. Yet, admitting your failures if and when they come and reacting fast is a key trait that has become essential to most Seed and series A VCs' decision process[2].

---

[2] Refer to chap 4: 'Entrepreneurs and adaptability quotient'

Mindset is an essential quality in the startup world. Before hiring someone, don't just look at their resumé: test their mindset.

When you present to your board, don't just prepare a set of intentions; come with KPIs that will show what worked and what didn't work and your actions to fix and enhance.

When you go to a meeting with a giant, don't sell yourself short, ever: adopt a winning mindset so you will win.

'Act as if.'

Plot summary
- ☐ Think about the value you will bring to your customers, work on your USPs
- ☐ Accelerate with the learnings of your failures
- ☐ Choose the people who will surround you, test the mindset of the people you hire

Ready, set, action!
- ☐ What were your recent failures? What did you learn from them?
- ☐ What are you most scared of? How can you manage it?
- ☐ How do you choose the people you surround yourself with? Do you feel exhilarated or dragged when you leave a meeting?
- ☐ What is your vision? How far can you see?

CHAP 2: CREATE & ITERATE YOUR VALUE PROPOSITION

Masterchef Mystery Box[3]

In the Masterchef TV show[4], there is a well-known segment called the mystery box challenge. The concept is that chefs must create an amazing recipe from ingredients they know nothing about.

This challenge represents a striking parallel with the startups' world. Given the wrong ingredients to begin with, CEOs struggle with the writing of their value proposition.

---

[3] Photo by Vladimir Proskurovskiy on Unsplash
[4] MasterChef is an American competitive cooking reality TV show based on the British series of the same name, open to amateur and home chefs.

Where do you start? How do you make it simple enough that anyone sees value instantaneously? How do you know it is the right one?

First things first, the foundations: your value proposition relies upon two main ingredients, both of which turn around the problems your solution solves.

1. What issues will you fix for your customers?
2. How do you address these issues better than anyone else?
3. How well do you know the market you will address?

If your value proposition doesn't highlight these two elements with transparency, go back to rewriting it. You are missing the essence.

Call your ideal customers and ask them why they bought from you in the first place. Try to understand in granular details their pains, why they acted, and why they chose you rather than someone else. However, there is a catch here. You may hear that they have chosen your company... because you were cheap—this is the cold shower. At least, you know, and you can act on it. [5]

The second part you must focus on is why you are 'better than anyone else' and there might be several reasons, most likely inherent to your original vision. For example, you might be the only one to do what

---

[5] Refer to chap 12: pricing strategy and margin

you do, or you may educate a market in doing things differently. It does not matter whether you have twenty-five competitors or none, the point is, if people buy from you, there is a reason, and that reason is called a differentiator or a unique selling proposition.

We naturally distinguish three types of differentiators.

The unique differentiators:
Your solution has unique features that no other competition big or small can compare too. Your Unique Selling Proposition (USPs) might be a combination of features, for example, you can match all your competitors' features but at scale, or on SaaS, or with fast deployment.
Unique differentiators have a life expectancy. As soon as they are available to the general public, they will be copied.

The comparative differentiators:
You provide similar features to other vendors, but you deliver them differently, with more execution, more details.

The holistic differentiators:
These are quite particular in the sense that they combined everything that you are, your essence except for your product, your technology. When all your holistic differentiators are combined into a story: vision, VCs, expertise, customers, people, ... with passion; it is an incredible pitch to diverge from

feature functions discussions. It inspires anyone to work with you rather than anyone else.

Last, assess your market knowledge. If you are a startup entrepreneur, you are disrupting a market somehow. This means that you will be educating your customers on new ways of doing things. To achieve this, you must appear as the expert, own their market Key Performance Indicators, and how you can influence them. Ask yourself: how do my potential customers measure themselves? And if they don't, how should they?

Now let's imagine you are at the comfortable stage where you feel delighted with your current value proposition, and it is, indeed, in alignment with the elements listed above. The work doesn't end here! A value proposition is never set in stone, do the following actions on a regular basis.

Check out the competition:
Do they use the same words? Do they have similar 'differentiators'? Is your value proposition truly unique? To avoid competing, you must stand out from the competition and, if you are disrupting an old industry, be different from the long-established contenders.

Be aware of external changes:
Customer behaviors and trends evolve, new regulations appear, your environment changes. COVID-19 has been one of those major external

changes that have shaken any company, small or big, to review and rewrite their value proposition.

Spread out your wings and vision:
The more you sell, the more you learn about the use cases you address and the results your customers have obtained. Meanwhile, your R&D continues to develop new features that bring more value and expand your vision. Don't get stuck. As you evolve, your value proposition must evolve too, taking both customer facing and R&D progression into account.

Reuse and upcycle:
Your value proposition can be easily declinable per persona. Use your core messaging and modify it accordingly for each department you wish to address, adapting to their different perspective on priorities. A CFO's focus tends to be cost reduction and optimization, while a CTO cares more about innovation and go-to-market. Don't make your life harder than it needs to be.

Think Macaroons! The recipe is the same for all, you may want to change the color and filling slightly, but you don't want to reinvent a whole new recipe every single time, especially if you get your macaroons right.

In summary, when it comes to writing and assessing your value proposition, keeping it simple is essential. Answering a problem your customer has in a way no one else does with quantifiable business impact is crucial. Ensuring your value proposition evolves as your company does is imperative.

Plot summary
- ☐ Address a problem and a market.
- ☐ Know the market you address, be an expert and educate your customers.
- ☐ There are 3 types of differentiators: Unique, Comparative and Holistic.
- ☐ Be aware of external changes.
- ☐ Spread out your wings and vision.
- ☐ Reuse and upcycle.

Ready, set, action!
- ☐ What KPIs will your solution/company have an impact on? List your differentiators on a white page: what do you do that no one else does?
- ☐ Associate pains/ problems you address to each feature listed on your roadmap; does it match?
- ☐ Do your features on the roadmap solve actual business problems such as reducing cost, increasing revenue or reducing risk?

CHAP 3: STOP PITCHING, EVEN IF YOU'RE CEO

Star Wars[6]

As a founder, you may have dreamed, like Anakin Skywalker, that one day, you would become the most powerful Jedi ever. You have the vision and charisma required to transport your potential clients to the promising land and live in infinite glory together.

Han Solo: 'Great kid. Don't get cocky.'

Yet, this promising land offers so many new possibilities that it appears unreachable. Yet after such a meeting of wonders, the magnetic CEO

---

[6] Photo Credit: Rosie Kerr on unsplash

cannot comprehend why nothing happens after that. No deep dive, no demo, in fact, no response to emails from the people her or she has met. Let's call it… the Sarlacc Pit.

C-3PO: 'In his belly, you will find a new definition of pain and suffering, as you are slowly digested over a thousand years.'

If, when you leave the meeting, you feel like you've won the Clone Wars, then, in reality, something definitely went wrong.

Obi-Wan Kenobi: 'Be mindful of your thoughts, Anakin. They will betray you.'

Let me explain what just happened: your prospect is indeed impressed by your **product** but has no clue how it relates to his/her daily operational way of working. As a result, your prospect will not engage any further time nor resources in your consideration.

Han Solo: 'You've never heard of the Millennium Falcon? It's the ship that made the Kessel run in less than 12 parsecs.'

Picture the Millennium Falcon. Yes, it is the fastest vessel in the Star Wars canon. Still, not everyone is capable of buying it, renting it, let alone piloting it.

Han Solo: 'Traveling through hyperspace ain't like dusting crops, farm boy. Without precise calculations, we could fly right through a star or bounce too close to a supernova, and that'd end your trip real quick, wouldn't it?'

It is not that your solution is not good enough. In fact, it is the opposite. Your solution appears almost too excellent because you are **pushing** it down the throat of your potential buyer.

Yoda: 'That is why you fail.'

Instead, you should have **pulled** information. You failed. To become a potential partner, you mustn't be missing out on a significant conversation. Listen, qualify further your understanding of why and how, your prospect will need you.

The first thing you should do with a potential buyer is to **get to know him**. And when I say that, I do not mean to ask mundane and meaningless questions that will bring no value to your interlocutor but will only make him feel like he's under an examination.

Qui-Gon Jinn: 'The ability to speak does not make you intelligent.'

The ability to ask open-ended questions and listen might make you so. If you have done a bit of research: read the annual report when available, browse the website, press releases, and check the LinkedIn profile of the people you are going to meet. With this, you should have some conversation openers.

Anakin Skywalker: 'Sometimes, we must let go of our pride and do what is requested of us.'

There is a reason why trilogies work. Combining open-ended questions with empathy and analytics before talking about your solution, will allow you to fully align with your prospect current situation. It is easier and more likely to be receptive to a technology's benefits if your prospect perceives a way in which you can solve their problems. A path to engage in deeper conversations with more resources will open.

Jyn Erso: 'Trust goes both ways.'

This is why, when you meet a prospect, no matter how good, how disruptive and incredible your solution is, refrain from talking about it. There are a thousand ways of positioning yourself – you know very well your solution offers more than one use case and you want to choose the right one.

Dooku: 'The acceptance of others is not a guarantee. Like everyone else, a Jedi is accepted or not based on his behavior. The Jedi who believes that he is more important than others only demonstrates that his opinion is to be ignored.'

So here are a few steps to follow:

First, secure your position as a trusted advisor by showing your knowledge of their company. This can be done by engaging on the business strategies you've read in their annual report, commenting on a recent press release, or even using a recent tweet as a conversation starter.

Second, show genuine interest, take them down a trench of open-ended questions, TED questions (tell me, describe to me, explain to me…). Your potential customer may then realize the issues and associate potential business impacts. These conversations are what differentiate you from being a simple supplier and ultimately transform you from a simple Padawan to a customer approved Jedi.

Gold Five: 'Stay on target'

Last and last only, start talking about yourself, your story, why you created your solution, and your company in ways that resonate with your prospect's current situation. Use your prospect's own words. Create the will to work with you by engaging them in an alliance. Before the end of the meeting, secure their engagement by asking for a purposeful next step to solve their issue.

Han Solo: 'I used to wonder about that myself. Thought it was a bunch of mumbo-jumbo: a magical power holding together good and evil, the dark side and the light. The crazy thing is… it's true. The Force. The Jedi… All of it… It's all true.'

Put the plan in motion. Practice and practice some more. It will not be easy at first. The urge to talk about the solution you've been developing, cooking, and loving will burn you at times. Refrain.

Yoda: 'You must unlearn what you have learned.'
Whatever happens, Yoda says *'Do. Or do not. There is no try.'*

Once you have started, check your metrics:

- Is your pipeline growing?
- Do you convert more first meetings into opportunities?
- Do you increase the average size of your opportunities?

To measure your success, you may want to monitor for the following short term KPIs:

- Average new deal size
- Average new deal length
- Conversion discovery to next step

In the long run, this new method should have an impact on:
- Customer Retention and churn rates
- Customer lifetime value
- New and expansion of Monthly Recurring Revenue (MRR)

And once you have learned, once you have proven, once you have secured long term clients…

Obi-Wan: 'The Force will be with you always.'

Plot summary
- ☐ Failing to prepare is preparing to fail.
- ☐ Combining open-ended questions with empathy and analytics is key to ensure a higher conversion rate.
- ☐ Attach your solution to their biggest business pains (and possibly personal pains).

Ready, set, action!
- ☐ Do you, as a CEO, go to all sales meetings? Do you have to be?
- ☐ How do you conduct your discovery?
- ☐ How do you prepare for a meeting? Do you feel that you know enough about your prospect? What are their main corporate objectives? Business Strategies?
- ☐ How will you identify and implicate a problem you may solve?

CHAP 4: ENTREPRENEURS & ADAPTABILITY QUOTIENT

Jurassic Parc[7]

In the startup world, there is a type of quotient that is more important for the survival of the startup species: the adaptability quotient[8].

You may have an astonishing Intelligence Quotient (IQ) and coded the most incredible software. You may have a prodigious Emotional Quotient (EQ) to win over a network of partners and customers in no time. Yet, when it comes to scale and exit, the Adaptability Quotient (AQ) is what a startup's executive management will require to excel truly.

---

[7] Photo by Fausto García on Unsplash
[8] Note that there are - to date- no formal ways of measuring the adaptability quotient yet.

Alan Grant: 'Dinosaurs and man, two species separated by 65 million years of evolution, have just been suddenly thrown back into the mix together. How can we have the slightest idea of what to expect?'

Great, so talent acquisition just needs to recruit people and Venture Capitalists (VCs) invest in CEOs with high AQ, to guarantee the success of the venture! After all, this is exactly what Nathalie Fratto[9] TedEd, speaker and investor at Goldman Sachs, does. Sounds easy enough, only how do you evaluate someone's AQ exactly?

Ian Malcom: 'How do you know they're all female? Does somebody walk into the enclosure and look under the dinosaur's skirt?'

In 2012, Jo Ayoubi[10], CEO and co-founder of Track surveys, outlined four main factors of the Adaptability Quotient:

- Ability to appreciate when change is happening (or even before it starts) and respond swiftly.
- Capacity to test and experiment promptly and often with products, services, business models, processes, and strategies.

---

[9] '3 ways to measure your adaptability— and how to improve it - Natalie Fratto'
[10] 'Adaptability is critical for successful organizations – but how adaptable is HR? HRmagazine.co.uk

- Ability to recognize and effectively manage stakeholders in complex relationships and roles.
- Capacity to motivate and lead in a rapidly changing environment.

The good news is that most of these skills can be taught and honed with practice over time. Some people have them naturally, although most of us will need to work for it. The first thing you should do is teach your brain to think in 'what if scenario'.

Much like playing chess, it forces your brain to be ready to act and react hastily, thus giving you an undeniable advantage when changes do materialize.

Ian Malcolm: 'If there's one thing the history of evolution has taught us, it's that life will not be contained. Life breaks free, it expands to new territories, and crashes through barriers painfully, maybe even dangerously, but, uh, well, there it is.

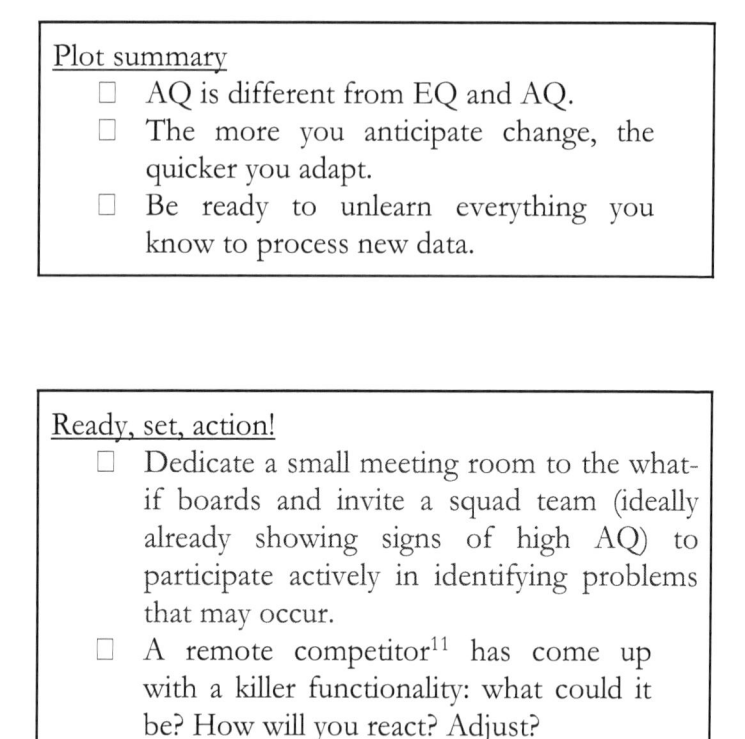

> Plot summary
> - AQ is different from EQ and AQ.
> - The more you anticipate change, the quicker you adapt.
> - Be ready to unlearn everything you know to process new data.

> Ready, set, action!
> - Dedicate a small meeting room to the what-if boards and invite a squad team (ideally already showing signs of high AQ) to participate actively in identifying problems that may occur.
> - A remote competitor[11] has come up with a killer functionality: what could it be? How will you react? Adjust?
> - Your top three spenders are churning for economic reasons, what will you do?
> - The opportunistic inbound sales have stopped drastically, you have no pipeline, your sales team is miserable: what will you do?

---

[11] See chapter 22: Fight the competition

CHAP 5: NO BULLYING & SAFE CULTURE

The Karate Kid[12]

In Karate Kid, Daniel LaRusso was bullied. He sought Karate training not to win but to defend himself. In business, I have been bullied. You have been bullied. Train to fight, so you won't have to.

There was a time when making business was governed by the law of the strongest. Success was dictated by how much power and how much control you exerted.

Large software established companies that don't need to be named have made their entire fortune by bullying their customers with tricky usage conditions,

---

[12] Photo by Leslie Jones

changes to terms, and any time of pressure to avoid churn. This is what, unfortunately the Cobra Kai sensei John Kreese was teaching his students in Karate Kid, failing to provide them with the bigger picture.

John Kreese: 'We do not train to be merciful here. Mercy is for the weak. Here, in the streets, in competition: a man confronts you. He is the enemy. An enemy deserves no mercy.'

Nevertheless, in an era when the subscription model has become the standard[13], this attitude is, thankfully, no longer trendy nor acceptable to anyone. SaaS companies are rising above money-driven bullying tactics, putting the customer experience at the heart of their business strategies, caring for them to encourage retention and avoid churn. The startup business should and can be one of benevolence and mutual aid. Plus, let's put it bluntly: bullying, even in business, is bad for your Karma, and Karma is a bitch.

Mr. Miyagi: 'Then why train?'
Daniel: 'So I won't have to fight.'
Mr. Miyagi: 'Miyagi have hope for you.'

When looking at a situation from the outside, it is easy to recognize the persecutor from the persecuted. However, there might be a time when you will be asked to take aggressive actions that contradict your core values. The motivations will be stronger than

---

[13] Refer to Chap 19: 'Sales process in the subscription era'

you had ever imagined: you may want to keep your job, offer your company the chance to make it through another quarter, obtain a large investment, or hire the people you've dreamed of…

Kreese: 'Sweep the leg. Do you have a problem with that?'
Johnny: 'No, Sensei.'
Kreese: 'No mercy.'

Bullies have the inner talent to uncover your apparent weaknesses and use them to make you do things you would not never consider. Sometimes, they can make you a bully yourself.

It can be incredibly hard to hide all your business weaknesses, know that you can turn them into strengths by looking at them from another perspective.

Imagine you are low on cash, and a potential investor is pushing you around? Turn to your most loyal customers for a potential upsell, prepayment, or even investment. Tell the truth to your initial investors for support…

Maybe the issue is different: you have signed an abusive clause in a contract. You could try to figure out an unseen exit strategy with your most trusted advisors.

Mr. Miyagi: 'Problem: attitude.'
Daniel: 'No the problem is, I'm getting my ass kicked every other day. That's the problem.'

Mr. Miyagi: 'Hai, because boys have bad attitudes. Karate for defense only.'

The more you comply with bullies against your will, the worse your situation will become. Assess and reassess the people you surround yourself with.

As a CEO, meticulously consider your future investors not just on the cash and timesheet quality, go further: check their credentials, their reputation, the support they can provide you, seek out stories of how they've backed up some of their startups under high pressure. Make reference calls. VC lawyers have seen it all and have a deep understanding of the ecosystem.

As a future co-founder, carefully select who you will be sharing the company's creation with. A character assessment is not to be overlooked.

As a future new employee, remember that the interview goes both ways. Are you completely comfortable with the new leadership you will be joining and working under?

As a customer or a partner, can you tell whether the win-win relationship you see will last and grow in time?

There are no bad decisions, only poor choices.

Mr. Miyagi: 'No such thing as bad student, only bad teacher. Teacher say, student do.'

Nevertheless, despite all your efforts you might still find yourself bullied in business. In this particular event, there are three potential exits: **Accept, Quit or Improve.**

--Accept--

It is a temporary option until you find a better solution.

--Quit--

The most comfortable position, one that I have personally chosen several times. It is not the coward's option when you do not have the strength in that moment to do better. However, it is never the long-term solution.

--Improve--

In most situations, the bullies have a motive for bullying. By finding out the root cause of the problem, you can fix it. Often, it is anchored in fear. Fear of making the wrong investment and wrongly believe they can fix it by exercising control. Find the root cause, control it, fix it, improve the situation.

Daniel: 'When do I learn how to punch?'
Mr. Miyagi: 'Better learn balance. Balance is key. Balance good, karate good. Everything good. Balance bad, better pack up, go home. Understand?'

The most important question is also the most difficult one. Do you have the capacity to put your bully back on **the right path**? Can you let go of the offense, of the aggression, and offer a collaborative exit? Can you close the loop so that this bully not only stops bullying you but also anyone else? Can you start a ripple effect?

Mr. Miyagi: 'Fighting always the last answer to problem.'

Disclaimer:
As a female writer and leader, I had the option to look at the male-female dynamic. Bullying has no place in business, in the workplace, on the school playground. It has no place, anywhere. Period.

Plot Summary
- ☐ You may find yourself in a position where you are the bully because someone else puts you to, stay true to yourself.
- ☐ You have three choices when found in a bullied or uncomfortable work position: accept, quit, improve.
- ☐ Try to put the Bully back on the right track.

Ready, set, action!
- ☐ How can you prevent a bullying culture?
- ☐ Are you certain that the new talents joining your team are sharing your core value?
- ☐ When it comes to investors, do you look at the timesheet, the money, the conditions...and the people?

CHAP 6: SEGMENT & CHOOSE YOUR FIRST CUSTOMERS

Back to the Future II

You know the drill, Doc and Marty get in their time machine once again, but this time, they head to the future. During their short stay, Marty has the inspired idea of buying a sports almanac, which would give him access to all the scores, results, and winning teams of the last twenty years (or, when he returns to his present, the next 20).

What if, as a CEO, you could predict who to bet on, when to do it and how?

To know who you should bet on, you must define your go-to-market strategy. Startups are -and should be- proud of their technology. Yet, in the SaaS B2B world, the technology is as good as the potential volume of customers it will serve. To start with a solid foundation of your Total Addressable Market (TAM), you must define as early as possible who your best prospects are and why they are a perfect match.

Most startups in Europe start generating revenue in an opportunistic manner (inbound leads[14], network and personal connections, mass mailing...), while startups in the USA focus from their very early stage on who they should win first.

Doc: 'Where we're going, we don't need roads'

To identify who you should target to begin with, don't stop at the obvious criteria such as vertical sector or number of employees. Instead, check that your vertical of predilection is the easiest for you to win, one where you will be solving a problem with high value. In the vertical and size company range alone, not all companies will be an immediate match.

Spend some time sorting who the early adopters are in your field, who has invested in new technologies, who is more prone to start new programs.

Understand their business and IT situation and search the people they have recruited to implement

---

[14] Inbound leads are, by definition, customers knocking on your door either because of marketing campaigns, SEOs, or network and community recommendations.

their strategies. With this information in mind, you will be more relevant, offering more value from the first meeting thus accelerating your average time to close and increasing your average size deal.

'If you put your mind to it, you can accomplish anything.'

This study may take you more than a couple of weeks to create, it is essential to lay out your go-to-market strategy before putting it to execution. The idea here is not to spend time in theory land, yet by writing your business roadmap you will convert more and at a higher rate.

You must readjust your segmentation on a regular basis with external factors or any new economics, politics, competition situation.

Execute it as soon as you can on the field, to test it and assess its validity. You must identify where you are relevant, where you are not, and why.

To start testing your strategy, you must:

1. Take the time to make assumptions based on the current data at your disposal.

2. Identify a list of KPIs to monitor for additional insight:

- ☐ Inbound leads vs. Outbound leads[15] (#)
- ☐ Average sales cycle (time)
- ☐ Average size deals (€)
- ☐ Number of deals per quarter (#)
- ☐ Time to close the first deal (weeks/months)
- ☐ Smallest deals vs. Biggest deals

3. Be ready to adjust on a quarterly basis.

Doc Brown: 'Your future hasn't been written yet. No one has. Your future is whatever you make it. So, make it a good one.'

If you take too long to figure things out, you may lose your perfect match to the competition or one of the bigger vendors consolidating a large contract. Now, the tricky question is, when should you invest time and resources in such a plan?

As early as possible and as often as your strategy evolves, which in the startup world is...often. Technology is important, but only if you have the right go-to-market strategy. How many times have you witnessed a startup losing market share to another one with an average technology and a perfectly well executed go-to-market strategy?

---

[15] Outbound leads are customers you have contacted.

- ☐ Execute on your strategy.
- ☐ Establish your ideal prospects list.
- ☐ Engage with them as soon as possible.

The next step is to facilitate your plan's execution by laying out how your startup is more relevant than anyone else to solve the problems (USPs). Marketing, R&D and sales must own the 'how' to align and reach 88mph!

Plot summary
- ☐ Find out your ideal prospects based on at least 5 criteria.
- ☐ Measure yourself to make adjustments.
- ☐ Test drive your strategy on a quarterly basis.

Ready, set, action!
- ☐ How well do you know your segmentation? How much thought have you or your team put into it? Is it documented and shared across the departments?
- ☐ Do you feel you are still doing opportunistic sales?
- ☐ Who are your best existing customers and why? Have you listed the criteria? What were their reasons for buying?

CHAP 7: PROSPECTING MASTERPLAN

The Hunger Games

Reaching out to prospects, gaining their attention and converting them is one of the most challenging parts of the business. Much like the hunger games, successfully mastering this game requires fire and resilience.

I may attract the wrath of many when I stand by the following statement: when it comes to prospecting, pure cold calling is no longer effective, especially in 2020. The last role you want to embrace for your own good is the one of the people who calls at the worst time of the day to… sell something. It's not about protecting your ego; it's about putting your company reputation and value on the right stand from the very first touchpoint. For this you should work on warm calling.

Katniss Everdeen: 'I volunteer! I volunteer! I volunteer as tribute!'
Effie Trinket: 'I believe we have a volunteer.'

Step 1: Do your segmentation[16] and re-iterate quarterly.

Effie Trinket: 'Happy Hunger Games! And may the odds be ever in your favor.'

Step 2: Learn everything there is to know about your target market.

If you've done your segmentation right, you should not have more than thirty companies to target for the ongoing quarter. Your early adopters will top a maximum of twenty-five accounts (enterprise) up to a hundred (mid-market).

You must secure the first wave of early adopters before moving forward to the second wave who require references and credibility to engage with a startup.

When an annual report is available, make sure to read it and understand it to attach yourself to the corporate objectives and business strategies of the company you are meeting. Follow the press and add Qwant, Google, LinkedIn, Twitter notifications to new initiatives. Use them as ice breakers even if you are not directly concerned or impacted by the news.

---

[16] Refer to Chap 6: Segment and choose your first customers.

Step 3: Identify the personas

Knowing about an account is good. Knowing who you should meet and talk to at the prospect is even better. Follow the pains you address to discover the personas who own them.

Make a list and follow them on social media platforms, add them to the sales navigator. Know what they are up to professionally, who they are connected to, and what they like. If the information is made public by these personas, they will appreciate your interest.

Peeta Mellark: 'I remember everything about you. You're the one that wasn't paying attention.'
Katniss Everdeen: 'I am now.'

Step 4: Be human

'People buy from people' is still a true statement, even in the digital age, and especially during the pandemic.

Robots have yet to replace the role of sales. The human touch is crucial to develop a meaningful relationship. Without trust, there is no moving forward. Build trust early on and make sure it lasts beyond just one opportunity; make sure your reputation as a trustworthy person follows you wherever you go in your career.

Engage with people you are selling to in much the same way you would at a social event. Find common topics, give them attention, maybe even compliment them in the most respectable and trustworthy way. This is what is commonly called 'the Art' in selling, use your emotional quotient.

When you finally interact with them through a call or over Zoom, ask them open-ended questions in the most natural way. Connect.

Cinna: 'Why don't you just be yourself? ... No one can help but admire your spirit.'

Now that we've established the foundations to build up a healthy prospecting plan, what's next? Prospecting is never a linear process. It is a spider web you frame with technique and skills. To successfully achieve your prospecting plan, you will require allies.

Haymitch Abernathy: 'You really wanna know how to stay alive? You get people to like you. When you're in the middle of the games, and you're starving or freezing, some water, a knife or even some matches can mean the difference between life and death. And those things only come from sponsors, and to get sponsors, you have to make people like you.'

Step 5: Find your allies

Marketing: Do not wait for your marketing department to drive traffic to your website and create Marketing Qualified Leads (MQL) or inbound leads. Your B2B acquisition cost will climb up to the roof if you do not apply the same segmentation to your marketing strategy.

B2B acquisition, events, and content marketing should align with your go-to-market strategy. When you know who you are targeting, you also own the type of content that should be relevant. Your marketing department can then focus and create the expected content: case studies, testimonials, and webinars titles that will catch the attention of the right people.
The more you own your vision, the more marketing will enable it. Whoever is in charge of sales is responsible to write that vision and participate in it.

Partners: We commonly distinguish two types of partners, technology partners and service partners.

- Technology partners are companies you associate with on the product side. Typically, you would provide a complementary end to end offer with an API integration. Technology partners will accelerate your growth by giving you access to their customer portfolio. This is a way for them to boost their revenue through upsell and, for you, to penetrate their market.

Technology partners usually have access to the high-level executive. They have already engaged and negotiated with them. Knowing your accounts and the persona you target will accelerate your relationship with the partners and a better understanding of the overall value (not just a tech solution) you bring to the table.

Technology partners allow you to gain credibility and represent a potential exit strategy for your startup.

☐ Deployment/ services partners enable your solution when your service team is too small, overwhelmed or not recruited yet. They are also quite valuable when you wish to focus your resources on annual recurring revenue (ARR) rather than service revenue.

These partners have eyes and ears in all parts of the companies you target. They know the operations well, their functional pains and the politics. Giving them guidance on why you should target some of these accounts can lead to a warm introduction and possible common business opportunities.

Katniss Everdeen: 'Great. Now I have to go back and tell Haymitch I want an eighty-year-old and Nuts and Volts for my allies. He'll love that.'

All of the above represents a clear picture of how you should own your prospecting plan and execute it. Not half, not a third, all of these actions are necessary to successfully master your prospecting plan and a successful pipeline creation.

- ☐ Analyze your segmentation
- ☐ Stay on top of your targets' current affairs
- ☐ Network with partners,
- ☐ Leverage marketing resources relentlessly
- ☐ Provoke regular touchpoints on social selling.
- ☐ Craft VITO[17] (Very Important Top Officer) letters followed with close connections with personal assistants

What is the conversion rate of a potential prospect after sending a non-crafted email? Answer: less than one percent. Isn't it time to work on your return on time invested?

Haymitch Abernathy: 'This is the time to show them everything. Make sure they remember you.'

Once you've found your way in, the rest is up to you.

Katniss Everdeen: 'Thank you for your consideration.'

---

[17] Selling to VITO the Very Important Top Officer: Get to the Top. Get to the Point. Get to the Sale by Anthony Parinello.

Plot summary
- [ ] Create, document and share a prospecting plan. Execute it
- [ ] Segment your customers and get to know them
- [ ] Identify the personas and how to connect
- [ ] Connect with allies through marketing and partners

Ready, set, action!
- [ ] What format do you use to track your prospecting plan?
- [ ] How do you measure your prospecting achievements?
- [ ] How do you know when your strategy works or does not work and how to readjust?
- [ ] Who have you socialized your plan with?

BOOK II

BUILD IT UP

CHAP 8: AVOID THE BURN OUT

Home Alone[18]

The issue of maintaining a proper Work Life Balance for the entrepreneur is a topic that remains unspoken for many. To remind all of us that personal hygiene, sleep, and healthy food is a must to function well, we will use the example of a special someone who was once alone for Christmas: Kevin McCallister from Home Alone.

Becoming an entrepreneur has its many challenges. It's like you've entered the grown-up world at an

---

[18] Photo Credit Mike Blank

accelerated pace unmeasurable by the human eye. One day you're sitting by yourself with a great idea, and the next, you're surrounded. A new crowd of people demands your time: investors and their money to spend wisely, customers and their revenue to cash in while maintaining their satisfaction; and a bunch of new people to take care of; your employees, who, let's face it, are the kids you did not plan to have.

Kevin: 'This is my house. I have to defend it.'

It is understandable that to remain afloat; you cut down on some of the basics such as time for yourself, including healthy food, sports, meditation, personal reading, and family time. Simple enough?

Wait?! Are you *really* doing this?

Kevin: 'Bless this highly nutritious microwavable macaroni and cheese dinner and the people who sold it on sale. Amen.'

The negative consequences of not letting go, not allocating this crucial, vital time in your calendar are following (non-exhaustive list):

1) Your brain will have trouble functioning properly to the best of its capacity.
2) Your emotions will blow out of proportion.

3) You may end up making poor decisions based on 1+2 that will take you more time to fix than if you had carved time for you and your family in the first place.

Kate (Kevin's mum): 'I have been awake for almost 60 hours. I'm tired, and I'm dirty. I have been from Chicago to Paris to Dallas to... where the hell am I?'

As an entrepreneur, you may see your body as a machine which serves your purpose: deliver. For the machine to function well, you must make sure to follow its primary requirements:

--Eat--

Let go of the nachos and chips. Forget the microwavables and the Deliveroos. Eat three proper meals a day with all the veggies and fruits you can get. Don't skip any: your busy brain requires all of them to function correctly.

Harvard Health recommends the following:

- Leafy green such as kale (I particularly like them with coconut oil to make chips in the oven!).

- ☐ Fatty fish such as salmon (which you can get as a sushi delivery)

- ☐ Berries improve memory and require no cooking.

- ☐ Walnuts (any nuts really) that you can keep by the computer or in your jacket pocket as a snack.

All of these included in your daily diet will assist you in fueling your brainpower.

--*Exercise*--

Some founders run, others do yoga, others sit and work on a chair 24/7.

At a minimum, give your body the chance to exercise 30mn a day, especially when working remote or from home. Walking 30 minutes can unlock issues and inspire new ideas.

'Many studies have suggested that the parts of the brain that control thinking, and memory (the prefrontal cortex and medial temporal cortex) have greater volume in people who exercise versus people who don't' says Heidi Godman from the Harvard Health letter.

--*Sleep*--

Studies show that the average person requires 7 to 9 hours to function well, although the acceptable low line lies at 6 hours. more than quantity of sleep, you must care about your sleep quality. Despite the numerous articles on the matter there are no clear guidelines or insights on what works best for entrepreneurs. For some, it is a routine. For others, catching up when they can, the point is: they make sleep work for them, not the other way around. Can't make it a minimum of six hours straight? Why not consider a power nap?

--*Hydrate*--

Coffee is not hydration!!! And remember that alcohol leads to dehydration.

--*Delegate*--

Doing everyone's job when you are five people in the company is not acceptable. When you are fifteen, it is not normal. When you are twenty-five or more, it is insanity and poor recruitment. Recruit talents, people that you trust, and learn to delegate.

The question is not so much if you know what is good for you but if you do apply these tips in your daily routine.

How many founders do respect all of the above? How many find their balance? When you add family members' attention, requirements and expectations to the mix, can you maintain a healthy rhythm? Not respecting these basics will lead you to unwanted emotions, frustrations, and possible outbursts.

If you have this under control already, perfect. Just be conscious that the passion you put in your startup and the counter-pressure it represents may create an unwanted gap with your personal life. Your vision may no longer align with your family, partner or friends' expectations. You may accept to lose people that are no longer part of your new world or, you may decide to take actions to include them more.

Kevin: 'I made my family disappear.'

Finally, one of the best resets of all times and best return on time invested for the busy entrepreneur is guided meditation. If you are a master at meditation, then this chapter was not for you in the first place, but if you are new to the concept, try to see if you can unwire for 3 minutes to get started... The benefits might get you addicted.

Kevin: 'I took a shower washing every body part with actual soap, including all my major crevices...including in between my toes and in my belly button, which I never did before but sort of enjoyed.'

Plot summary
- ☐ Find the balance that works for you.
- ☐ Find your eating, exercising, sleeping, hydrating and delegating rhythm.
- ☐ Make sure your entourage aligns with your goal and vice versa.
- ☐ Meditate.

Ready, set, action!
- ☐ How much personal time do you carve out a day? How do you manage for your entourage to respect it?
- ☐ Do you feel that some days are harder than others? Have you thought of using these days to take a break?
- ☐ How straightforward have you been with your friends and family on your aspirations and fears?
- ☐ How well do you delegate?

CHAP 9: THE QUESTION OF GOING FREEMIUM

Pretty Woman[19]

What is a freemium business model?

Freemium pricing is a business model, particularly found on apps, whereby basic services are provided free of charge. It is called Freemium in opposition to a Premium version which offers additional features or usage capacity at a cost.

When it comes to SaaS B2B, is a Freemium business model a sustainable go-to-market strategy? Are you sure you are not depreciating the value of your software, worth that, to your enterprise customer may be inestimable?

---

[19] Photo credit Colton Sturgeon

Edward: 'You can't charge me for directions!'
Vivian: 'I can do anything I want to baby, I ain't lost.'

Except maybe – there should be at least one exception to such a bold statement – if:

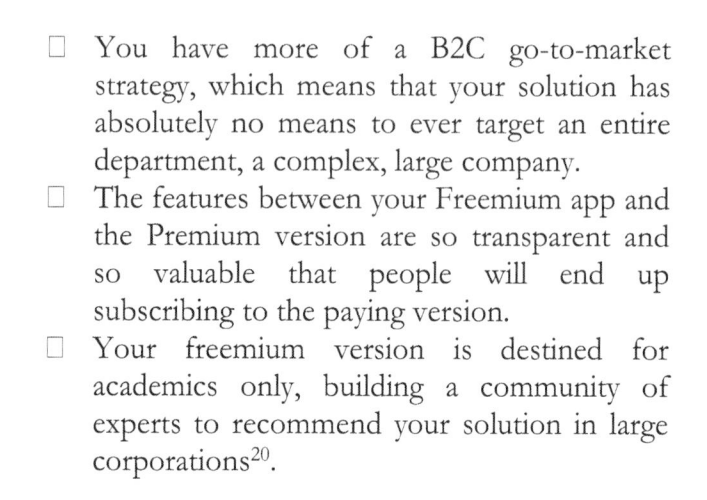

- You have more of a B2C go-to-market strategy, which means that your solution has absolutely no means to ever target an entire department, a complex, large company.
- The features between your Freemium app and the Premium version are so transparent and so valuable that people will end up subscribing to the paying version.
- Your freemium version is destined for academics only, building a community of experts to recommend your solution in large corporations[20].

Vivian: 'I appreciate this whole seduction thing you've got going on here but let me give you a tip: I'm a sure thing.'

Nevertheless, many startups believe that a Freemium offer is the way to go for growth and adoption at a very early stage. The main issue with thinking growth in your pricing strategy is that free volume will always equate to… zero dollars in the bank. And as we know, zero multiplied by one million is still zero, which is not helping your revenue growth. One million users paying nothing can leave you

---

[20] Benchling.Inc is a good example.

bankrupting your business in infrastructure, R&D and energy costs! Spotify[21], a B2C company lost €340M in 2019 with 265 Million users and 127 Million paying users.

Vivian: 'You people work on commission, right?'
Shop assistant: 'Yeah.'
Vivian: 'Big mistake. Big. Huge. I have to go shopping now.'

Before moving forward with any pricing strategy[22], you must do a little bit of homework:

Analyze your growth target audience:

- Who are you targeting, what type of population... are they price sensitive?
- What difference will you make in their day to day? What will be your stickiness?
- How can you become viral? How can you guarantee adoption?

Refine your product positioning:

- Is your software providing a solution that does not exist to a common problem?
- Is your platform based on features that no one else does?
- Is the product going to blow the users' minds from the first few hours of usage?

---

[21] Spotify Technology S.A. Announces Financial Results for First Quarter 2019 04/29/2019
[22] Refer to Chap 12: Pricing Strategy and Margin

With this in mind, you can define a value-based pricing strategy, one that will sustain your expansion.

Vivian: 'I never joke about money.'
Edward: 'Neither do I.'"

The common truth with a Freemium business model is that no matter how good your solution is, no matter how attractive the additional features might be, the person who is using your solution for free will do everything they can to keep it that way, especially if they can.

Vivian: 'I just wanna know who it works out for. You give me one example of somebody that we know that it happened for.'
Kit: 'Name someone? You want me to name someone? Oh, God, the pressure of a name... Cinde-fucking-rella!'

Except for Vivian and Cinderella, how many people really have the opportunity to leave the streets of Hollywood Boulevard and end up shopping on Rodeo Drive?

SaaS has brought new ways of doing business; prospects appreciate a short sales cycle as much as you do. Ensure that your user interface is a graphically mind blowing with practicality and that your solution is intuitive. With this, you can offer a limited trial, which could last up to two months to lock in your new customers with long term value.
With a solution that grabs the user's attention and solves a problem, you give yourself a chance to develop a relationship with your future customer.

Attempt a trial that requires a credit card sign up so that the user is automatically charged when the period is over instead of cutting the services.

Vivian: 'You know, you could pay me now, and break the ice.'

Your future is in your hands and mindset[23]. If you decide your company will be big, it will be. Never underestimate the value of what you are building. No empire was created by giving out software for free.

Carefully manage your customer lifetime value (LTV) to customer acquisition costs (CAC) ratio, or the payback period on your CAC.
Your scaling and employees' commitment depend on it.

'Welcome to Hollywood! What's your dream? Everybody comes here; this is Hollywood, land of dreams.' – Happy Man

---

[23] Refer to chap 4: Mindset Boost

Plot summary
- ☐ A Freemium business model is not for everyone. Consider your positioning and ask yourself if you have enough differences between your freemium app and premium to leverage paying customers.
- ☐ Consider a free limited trial instead of a freemium.
- ☐ Free never ever demonstrates high-end value.

Ready, set, action!
- ☐ What is your premium value?
- ☐ What will you achieve with a freemium solution that you would not achieve with a free trial?
- ☐ How are you positioning yourself? What is your plan to get the biggest deals in the large enterprise accounts?

CHAP 10: POC vs PILOT EXPLAINED

Would you let your grandfather teach you how to code? [24]

Unless your grandfather is Brian Kernighan, Richard Stallman, or even Linus Torvalds… Allowing a large corporation to tell you what to do when you are, by definition, writing the future in your area of expertise; is quite similar to letting your grandfather teach you to code.

Under the pressure and hope of closing a large corporation as a client, many startups will put up with providing resources they do not have to do a proof of concept (POC) that does not make sense. And, rarely, will they see an iota of money in return. This is because the prospects asking for POCs are rarely aligned with your ideal customer segmentation[25].

---

[24] Photo credit ThisisEngineering RAEng
[25] Refer to chap Chap 6: segment and choose your first customers

Nevertheless, you can still work with corporations when your business objectives are in alignment, which is often translated in a Pilot.

There is a great deal of difference between a POC and a Pilot, and it is important we understand the distinguishing terms of each to set the proper expectations for future collaborations.

A POC is acceptable when your product has not reached a minimum valuable product (MVP) and you require this step to build up your solution with field data. If your solution works technically, then you should avoid a POC at all costs. The reason is that 99% of POC are disposable side projects. At best, its result may end up as a dusty report on the corner of the C-levels desk. Rarely is it the beginning of a long-term partnership.

By accepting to move forward blindly with a POC, instead of opening the giants' eyes, educating them in the new ways of doing things, the startup downgrades its initial value to offer a simple commodity. This can only be the beginning of a frustrating relationship for both parties.

Under the investors pressure of winning new clients, the startup tries to fit in, accepting to fill out the RFP as it is written, when, in reality, they either turn it down or turn the table to rewrite it.

From the corporate giant perspective, they end up assuming based on the information available that they can do better in-house or with one of their existing vendors. Requests for Proposal (RFP) written by a corporation are limited. They lack the innovation skills and vision the startup could bring to the table.

A pilot, however, is inspired by the startup and its value proposition. By definition, it is the realization of a set of success criteria commonly agreed upon between the startup and the corporation. The objective of the pilot is to solve a business issue by defining the proper use case. The pilot shall then be governed by defined Key Performance Indicators (KPI) with executives' involvement. It is a valued and paid project, a smaller version of a potential future larger deployment, defined by a perimeter that will build the internal confidence required to further extend the program.

How do you put yourself in a pilot situation rather than a POC then?

Avoid the misleading paths. Corporations are naturally attracted to the world of startups. They will open their welcoming arms to you and even invite you to pitch to their innovation day. Do it! This is a great door opening to expand your network and visibility. You might win an award which you will then use in your story telling (holistic differentiator pitch[26]). Nevertheless, the chances of closing a deal from such an invitation are slim and here's why:

---

[26] Refer to chap 2: Create & iterate your value proposition

--Perception--

You are part of the kids' club. You are not established. You are invited to boost energy and creativity with your brilliant minds and bright ideas, yet no one believes you are capable of proper execution.

--Audience--

Rarely is it composed of the operational people that need you, aka the businesspeople, the field people. Unfortunately, your pitch will unlikely resonate, even if your value proposition is amazing.

--No use case--

Your pitch will be too general, and it is not your fault. You are going in with little insights. You will not be able to attach yourself to the functional and business pains, which means your pitch[27] will be made of benefits, making you appear as 'nice to have'.

When invited to meet with a giant, no matter the opportunity, make sure you complete your research to change the perception:

- ☐ Show that you are established by telling customer success stories.

---

[27] Refer to Chap 3: Stop pitching even if you're CEO

- Do not pitch your solution, tell a story, why you created your startup, what problems you wish to solve.
- Talk about your vision and where you want to take your customers in the future.

Target your audience and persona:

- Research the web.
- Ask your partners and investors about the corporation.
- Understand their problems and how you can address them.
- Read the annual report, the press, get as much information as you can, including personas you should target.
- Be relevant.

Inbound and Opportunistic wins are the reason you may find yourself under the request of a previously written RFP or request for POC.

If you've done your homework, you know what your ideal customer profile looks like. Anyone that is remotely outside of your criteria may divert you from your ideal match. If a large corporation is calling on your door, don't let them qualify you, instead, qualify if you are a match and why you should invest your time and resources with them: do they have problems, or are they browsing? Have they set up their mind on what they're looking for? Can you address their issues? Are the people contacting researchers or actors?

Write the use cases with the operational people by meeting them frequently, understanding their issues, digging into the business impact, and educate them on the path you can provide for them.

The relationship between startups and corporations is a work in progress. Nevertheless, it is the startups' responsibility to lead the way by never compromising on their vision. You will thus avoid R&D confusion, burning unnecessary cash and resources, and educating the giants on a new and positive way to modernize.

Plot summary
- ☐ Only do a POC when you are at the beginning of your product realization (before an MVP).
- ☐ POCs are only used to prove that a solution works.
- ☐ A pilot involves stakeholders, decision makers, a pricing model and KPIs.
- ☐ A pilot is the roadmap for a larger deployment.

Ready, set, action!
- ☐ Do you need to train your machine learning? Do you need data? What will you gain in doing a POC? There must be value on both sides.
- ☐ If someone asks you for a POC and your solution is in production at 3 or more customers what should you do? Are you ready to walk away from a non-early adopter type of prospect?

CHAP 11: NO CHAMPION, NO DEAL

Million Dollar Baby[28]

Million Dollar Deals are possible even for the early-stage startup. Much like anything, you need the mindset and the strategy. Maybe add to that a bit of technique. When it comes to making these types of deals, experienced Enterprise Sales in B2B will know one thing: you cannot do it alone.

Professional boxers fight across different weight classes during their career. Therefore, winning titles at multiple weight classes and becoming a champion across multiple divisions is a major achievement.

---

[28] Photo Credit NeONBRAND

--No champ, No deal--

When it comes to bringing home a deal that can make history and be a life changer for your startup, you must get yourself a sparring partner that has not only the characteristics of a champion but those of a multiple champion.

How do you find such champions?

Every meeting, every touchpoint you have with a prospect is an opportunity to find a diamond in the rough.

--Identify--

What are their traits, and how can you **identify** Champions?

Here are a few tips: champions are, by definition, the ones that instantly get the respect in the room, they take the lead in the meeting, **they drive the conversation**, they seem to win from the beginning. When you look at their LinkedIn profile, you may find out that they have implemented programs. Maybe they've even created and managed a center of expertise.

They have power and influence even if they may not be the ultimate decision-maker. More importantly, they have a personal reason to make your solution a priority. Either because your solution can help them solve a problem that has an impact on their personal life or simply because they've grasped the potential of your solution to make their career evolve.

'The hero and the coward both feel the same thing. But the hero uses his fear, projects it onto his opponent while the coward runs. It's the same thing, fear, but it's what you do with it that matters.' – Cus D'amato.

Your champion is therefore **driven by fear or ambition**. Nevertheless, finding a Champion is not enough to bring the title home, you've got the material to work with, but now, the sweating must begin with hours in the ring testing and developing.

--*Test*--

Whatever his weight category, a real champion will give you access to other people in the organization or to his boss, dry run key meetings, ask for business information that will differentiate you from the others. You move forward, securing your position, ensuring that you are not betting on just a coach or a seemore (someone who will show a lot of interest but is just there to learn not to buy. He will always want to "see more"). It is a defining moment when you get out of a simple vendor/supplier relationship and develop into a true partnership.

--*Develop*--

Train your champion to be stronger than the competition's Champion. If he is responsible for selling for you when you are not there, you are responsible for giving him/her the best arguments[29] to do so.

- **Why do the project?**
  - Which constitutes your prospects' functional problem (s) and associated business impacts.

- **Why do it with your solution?**
  - Your differentiators and USPs must be clearly explained.

- **Why do it now?**
  - The time must come from your customer. Your prospect must feel the urgency either because of cost piling or revenue loss or risk (security, band exposure, regulations). We typically call this urgency a compelling event.

'The fight is won or lost far away from witnesses—behind the lines, in the gym and out there on the road, long before I dance under those lights.' —Muhammad Ali

Much like professional boxers do, the ideal situation is to multiply the titles and the belts. Play your

---

[29] Commonly referred to as a 3 why document that your work in a blank page (no logo) with your champion.

prospect at different categories and multiply your champions so that you can neutralize the competition. If you started your campaign at the operational level, chances are you have found yourself a technical champion. However, many other champions can be found such business, digital, sometimes even a security champion.

The more, the merrier. Yet the Holy Grail of the million-dollar deals, the Heavy Weight of all champions is your Deal Champion. The one that has power and influence at the most executive level, sometimes even has access to the board. That type of champion can carry the deals from operational language to business language, top to bottom, counter objections, put him/herself at risk and bring the contract home for you.

'Once that bell rings, you're on your own. It's just you and the other guy.' — Joe Louis

People buy from people, and Champions are for life. Your Champions will use you to win as much as you will use them to bring the title home. This relationship goes beyond a company relationship, and when a Champion makes a move in his career, changes company, he or she will remain in contact. Down the line, you may make a lifelong professional friend.

Invest in your groundwork. Be a human who solves problems, a trusted advisor with empathy, and the deals will grow (and flow).

'The [temptation] for greatness is the biggest drug in the world.'
— Mike Tyson

Plot summary
- ☐ No Champ -> No Deal.
- ☐ Champion plan: Identify, Test, Develop.
- ☐ Beware of the seemore and coaches.
- ☐ The more champions, the stronger and larger your deal.
- ☐ Champions are for life.

Ready, set, action!
- ☐ How do you multiply stakeholders?
- ☐ How do you identify that one person will sell for you when you are not there?
- ☐ What is his or her personal gain/personal pain?
- ☐ Have you written a development plan?

CHAP 12: PRICING STRATEGY & MARGIN

Ocean Eleven[30]

In Chapter 9: the question of going Freemium; we initiated the fundamentals of a well-executed pricing strategy. Much like a good robbery, pricing execution takes planning.

With funding on the rise in Europe, startup founders forget the basics. It has become acceptable, if not normal, for a startup - no matter the series - to burn through cash. Worse still, it is commonly acknowledged that they might not be cash flow positive for… a while.

---

[30] Photo by Guido Coppa

Saul Bloom: "I can assure you, Mr. Benedict, that your generosity in this matter will not go overlooked."

And indeed, we now have several great unicorns in Europe. For many of them however, the valuation is more based on the amount of money raised rather than actual generated revenue. The press rather adorns investment rounds than testimonials of customer won.

Saul Bloom: 'You expect us to just walk out the casino with millions of dollars on us?'
Danny Ocean: 'Yeah.'

In the long run, bringing in steady revenue is fundamental. It is what makes a startup's exit excellent or average. Metrics such as churn rate, renewal rate, growth, average size, annual contract value, and largest annual contract value determine true potential, otherwise known as the total addressable market (TAM).

Note that the TAM has an evolution of its own. Great companies expand their TAM by enlarging their scope of action and influence.

Livingston Dell: 'They'll be watching you like hawks. Hawks with video cameras.'

As a founder, you must handle the pressure of:

- ☐ Winning customers and credibility.
- ☐ Recruiting exceptional talent at the right price
- ☐ Determining a long-term roadmap that will differentiate you from competition.
- ☐ Gaining additional market share.
- ☐ Managing cost-efficiently.

You can reduce pressure levels by thinking carefully about a sustainable pricing model early on one that shall remain steady to avoid potentially disappointing existing customers.

Terry: 'Who the hell is this?
Rusty: 'The man who's robbing you!'

Margin = revenue - cost

When your story begins, being cash flow positive seems like an impossible mission. However, it should be a goal at all times. Consider all of your costs – not just operating costs, but also recruitment, people, and scaling costs. Don't just rely on future funds. Manage your P&L on actual data[31] and accurate forecasting[32].

Danny: 'You gotta walk before you crawl.'
Rusty: 'Reverse that.'

---

[31] Refer to chap 15: The data driven company
[32] Refer to chap 14: Sales forecast accuracy

Ask yourself the tough questions.
- ☐ How many customers do you need at your average ARR to break even, to become profitable?

- ☐ Is this number of customers reachable? In a year? In 5 years? Ever?

- ☐ How many resources will you require?

- ☐ Do you measure other metrics than revenue and new logos quarterly?

- ☐ Have you appointed a gatekeeper, such as a sales operation professional, to guide you and your team in the proposal process?

- ☐ How will you invest in growing the customers that you have won and avoided churn? Is this expense (customer success/support) included in your price? Is it valued by your customer?

Danny: 'That's why we're going to have to be very careful. Very precise.'
Rusty: 'Mmm, well-funded.'

Customer Segmentation Issues
Price per user per unit (per server, per user, per... use case?) has become the standard. That's ok, provided you set it right.

Problem 1:

You arrive with a solution to disrupt an industry that has experience of doing things a certain way and is used to a certain price.

>Typical behavior:

You set a meager price that does not differentiate you from your 'old' competition, even if you bring more flexibility, more ease of use, more productivity, more digital, and more modernity to the table.

>Negative consequences:

You need to raise funds until you have won enough customers to break even, diluting your value further.

Danny: 'Thirteen million and you drive this piece of shit cross country to pick me up?'
Rusty: [sarcastically] 'Blew it all on the suit.'

Problem 2:
You arrive with a new solution that no one has ever used to solve problems they did not know existed. However, you must educate the market first on why they need you and what you will change for them.

>Typical behavior:

You guesstimate a price because of the lack of data.

Negative consequences:
The price is often set too low. This allows you to win customers in the short term but means you get caught up quickly by new competition, which does what you do better and faster. You then become a commodity.

Reuben: 'You guys are pros. The best. I'm sure you can make it out of the casino. Of course, lest we forget, once you're out the front door, you're still in the middle of the f***ing desert!'

When you set a price, you send a message to the entire market. It tells people who you are, your value, your current, and future positioning. It requires a profound transformation, even for a startup, to move from mid-market deals to enterprise deals. And the issue is rarely that the solution is not good enough or not scalable enough. Rather, the price is often plainly too 'cheap'.

Danny: 'Cause the house always wins. Play long enough, you never change the stakes. The house takes you. Unless, when that perfect hand comes along, you bet big, then you take the house.'

Everything is in the price per unit issue.

Yes, your solution is a SaaS solution, and as such, your customer pays for a service that includes bug fixes, updates, and upgrades. It does not, however, mean that all additional features and functions should be included by default. Some of these features (security, privacy, customer success) should be considered as renewable packaged options that allow for additional recurring revenue. The math is simple: to provide a service of quality, you must hire people – forward-thinking developers, caring expert customer success...all of whom are on an annual salary.

Rusty: 'You'd need at least a dozen guys doing a combination of cons.'

Industry secret: the ones who make it are never the ones offering the low-priced solutions. If you come in cheap, you are already at risk of churn. If you are inexpensive and bringing a lot of value you will regret it: soon enough, you will have some difficulties maintaining the required and expected level of service without raising money again. To maintain your value, set the price where it should be: high. It is as simple as that.

Rusty: 'I need the reason. Don't say money. Why do this?'
Danny: 'Why not do it?

<u>Plot summary</u>
- ☐ Your pricing should not change drastically as you scale.
- ☐ Think about your value and the future value to your customers early on in setting your pricing high.
- ☐ Don't fall for a 'everything' is in the per unit price mistake.

<u>Ready, set, action!</u>
- ☐ Create a war room and discuss with your executives: what is the best strategy in the long run?
- ☐ Is your average size deal too low? Do you know why?
- ☐ Are you cannibalizing future sales in a one size fit all pricing model?
- ☐ How can you sell as options?

CHAP 13: NEGOTIATIONS SKILLS

Pirates of the Caribbean[33]

Using Pirates as a means to address negotiating techniques is a bold move... After all, aren't Pirates thieves? Yet, there is much more to consider than motives to the art of negotiation. Take attitude, for example.

The more information the negotiator owns, the more he/she can assess the situation to make an educated decision and get out of tricky and unwanted complications. When it comes to compromises, even the most talented negotiators tend to let the adrenaline take over and stop the investigation.

---

[33] Photo credit Luke Southern

Yet, if you ever let yourself make assumptions, you may as well go straight to the gallows. The consequences can be terrible, including speculations, tensed relationships, unwanted escalations, and... bad decisions. As usual, if you are uncertain of what to ask, the key to all the treasure chests is the word: *why*. Why is this important to you?

Captain Jack Sparrow: 'Why Fight When You Can Negotiate?'

If you did not ask this question, you may assume the price is the most important factor of the transaction and 'negotiate' against yourself, lowering your price and value ahead of time when the most important issue might be elsewhere.

Captain Jack Sparrow: 'Not all treasure is silver and gold, mate.'

Our dreadlocked Captain may appear as if he was born under a lucky star, although if you analyze his actions carefully you will notice that he consistently mitigates his risk. Do you?

'Failure to prepare is preparing to fail.'

Before sending any proposal, make a list of your non-negotiables. As a startup, you feel the pressure to win every deal, every customer, and, like most pirates, you'd be willing to sell your family to close the deal. This is exactly the attitude that will lead you to poor trades.

Captain Jack Sparrow: 'The problem is not the problem. The problem is your attitude about the problem. Do you understand?'

Always start the negotiations with a better version than your best-case scenario. You can only go down from there. Too many times, startup owners are so scared of losing their prospects they'll send out their -almost- worst-case scenario, only you can never negotiate up.

The consequences of that are:

- ☐ You have no room for negotiations.
- ☐ You are putting your company's future at risk (Annual Contract Value below break-even, threatening your profit & loss, legal documents accepting clauses that are too risky …)
- ☐ You have not assessed why your prospect needs you and how you bring him the value.

Pirate tip: When two parties enter into a *parley*, there is always one that has more to lose than the others. In most cases, the startup will think they are the lesser contender.

WRONG. If you have made your discovery and build value phases right, you should be in a forceful position. If you haven't, then don't even enter the negotiation, or you may as well walk the plank.

Captain Jack Sparrow: 'Complications arose, ensued, were overcome.'

The negotiation ends when the papers are signed. Until then, again, never assume the deal is done. Remember, this is pirate territory. Any party, at any point, can come with additional requirements or misunderstandings.

Will Turner: 'You didn't beat me. You ignored the rules of engagement. In a fair fight, I'd kill you.'
Captain Jack Sparrow: 'That's not much incentive for me to fight fair, then, is it?'

Last-minute requests are often considered painful and lengthy and you think it puts your forecast accuracy at risk. As a startup, it is the moment you expedite all requests with blind approval to secure the deal. Your fear is taking over. You think that if you don't say yes to all, you may lose the deal. Well, do not say yes to all. Last-minute requests often mean new opportunities to grow your deal!

Lord Cutler Beckett: 'You're mad.'
Captain Jack Sparrow: 'Thank goodness for that, 'cause if I wasn't this would probably never work.'

Late requests almost always originate from additional requirements and or higher executives getting involved…and this is a good thing! You can grow the size of your deal by being curious about who is asking the questions, why it is important to that person, and what would be the consequences of not doing it. And the answer is rarely: lose the deal. Continue your discovery. By all means, do not pull out your sword!

Will Turner: 'This is either madness... or brilliance.'
Captain Jack Sparrow: 'It's remarkable how often those two traits coincide.'

Plot summary
- ☐ Start the negotiation high, with your better than best case scenario.
- ☐ Stick to your list of non-negotiables.
- ☐ The person who wins is the person who holds the most information.

Ready, set, action!
- ☐ Before going into a room of negotiation, have you taken the time to work on your list of non-negotiables, and the things you are willing to let go of?
- ☐ Have you done your homework? Do you have more information than the other guy?
- ☐ If you feel weak, what is your plan to improve your position?
- ☐ Are you ready to walk away if need be?

CHAP 14: SALES FORECAST ACCURACY

In watchmaking like sales forecasting, it's all about the methodology

In 2016, the Fondation de la Haute Horlogerie wrote a white paper[34] to define fine watchmaking with a documented methodology. Much like sales forecasting, fine watchmaking had remained a vague idea for too long. Yet the similarities between both processes are evident, it requires talent, art, and deep granularity.

The accuracy of the numbers is essential to any company's prosperity: it gains the investors' trust, allows the startup to spend wisely, and master a scaling plan at the right pace.

---

[34]https://www.hautehorlogerie.org/en/the-foundation/cultural-council/white-paper-on-fine-watchmaking/

Spot on forecast accuracy is usually 95% -105% of the called numbers at the beginning of the quarter vs closed won deals at the end of the quarter ratio. A gap of more than 10% below or above is considered non accurate. To the exception of major external events e.g.: 2020/COVID19, it usually reveals an issue in the deal qualification and assessment.

During forecast calls, sales leaders refer to these consolidated numbers as "the worst case", "the best case", and the "gut feel." But… forecast accuracy does not live in their gut. Only probiotics do! And indeed, when one relies on instincts only, things can go wild. The pressure of quarter ends can alter the natural (unlearned) behaviors and their reliability. At scale, this can translate by your sales, believing a deal will close when all signals are red.

This is why any company should consider the process of forecast accuracy as a science. Just like fine watchmaking, there are several criteria you can measure against to accurately determine the timing, the size of the deal, and its likelihood to 'close.'

--Pipeline (10-35%)--

This section of your forecast often covers the following categories in your sales cycle:

1- discovery: a phase in which SDRs and the sales team uncover the situation, problem, and impact.

2- deep dive: a time when your presales and sales are attaching a potential customized demo/workshop to the discovery meeting, taking the opportunity to dig into use cases.

The first mistake when calling a number is believing there is an opportunity when really, there is not (yet). To differentiate an opportunity from a simple warm lead, basics questions apply:

- ☐ Have you had a conversation with someone of influence (champion) who opens up about technical or functional issues?

- ☐ Do these difficulties (pains) ideally have a business impact? Are the people you talk to engaging in the next step to solving the existing problems?

With **a pain** implicated by the prospect strong enough to be associated with a **compelling event** (must be owned by an economic buyer, defines a specific date by which a direct response to a negative business pressure must happen, it is the reason to act), **a champion, and a defined series of next steps** commonly agreed upon with your prospect, you can create an opportunity.

--*Best case (40-70%)*--

This section of your forecast often covers the following categories in your sales cycle:

3- Technical validation: a time when you multiply actions such as an additional technical workshop, security workshop, reference calls to other customers to validate that your solution is the actual answer to the prospect functional problem.

4- Proposal: a moment when you have received a verbal agreement on your technical skills with a 'vendor of choice' validation and start working on the business proposal's details.

The best-case phase is crucial. You have paved the way to differentiate yourself from the first interactions. Now it is time to prove how you do it and how you do it better than anyone else.

--Be ruthless--

You would be surprised of where your follow up emails and slide deck may end up. Your direct interlocutors are rarely the ultimate decision-makers. When sending any type of documentation, ask yourself: Who could read this? Am I clear enough who has never met anyone in my company?

Document your value proposition: why do something, why do it with you rather than the others, why do it now. If you don't know this, if you have not worked this with your champion, do not expect your prospect to figure it out.

Make it simple, to the point. Use as much of the prospect's own vocabulary to ensure you will be understood anywhere in your prospect organization. Anything you send out from a follow up to a proposal must be understandable and digestible by anyone in the company.

The main issue with forecast accuracy is to call the 'when.' You alone cannot define the timeline. Quarter-end and discounts worked in the 1990s as a reason for prospects to sign. Decades of bad habits have taught your customer they can get said discounts even if the deal does not sign-in time. Do not perpetuate this. Do not train your customer to sign on the very last day of the quarter.

So, how else can you manage the close date?

If your customer has a functional problem with a measurable business impact, they should, in consequence, have identified a **compelling event** that constitutes a reason for them to act at or before a specific date to avoid further consequences. Attach yourself to the prospect's business impact and its timeline. What is the consequence of not solving it by a certain date? Increased cost? Loss in revenue? Sometimes, you may realize at the very early stage of your sales campaign that you will not manage to bring the deal within a specific quarter. Even if the news is unpleasant, you are better off knowing it early. Prepare to work with your champions on ways to overcome roadblocks, and you hunt for some short-term deals.

---Be Measurable---

Document all your proposals, emails, and slide deck with relevant metrics that you have collected during the discovery phase with your prospects. Simple data such as 'here is how long it takes you…', 'how many errors….', 'the cost of…', 'how we will measure progress…', can be quite effective in proving your understanding of the situation in a non-generic way, developing trust in your attention to their success.

--Commit (75-100%)--

This section of your forecast often covers the following categories in your sales cycle:

5-negotiation: if you've managed your campaign right this is not the time for paperwork. It is the time to adjust final roadblock around legal, procurement and budget conditions.

6-signature and close: the last agonizing moments of waiting for the entire set of paperwork necessary to 'close' the deal.

This is not a mere component of the forecast accuracy. The negotiation[35] can involve a lot more than just the pricing. Payment terms, legal conditions, security requirements, processes, and more are not to be overlooked. If you have a champion and a compelling event, you've started documenting all

---
[35] Refer to Chap 13: Negotiation skills

necessary steps in a shared document, also called 'external sequence of events', from the earliest moment of your opportunity. Doing this early avoids leaving all the 'paper process' necessity and negotiations to the last minute.

--Be present--

If you are not taking care of your prospect, someone else is. Be there, bring value at all levels. Be friendly and useful. Don't harass the legal or procurement department for information. Instead, suggest workshops and carefully chosen resources to assist. This will increase your knowledge of their internal process and the potential timeline risk. If you are not talking to at least one person per week in a deal that you have forecasted in the quarter, you have little chance of closing it.

--Be a partner--

You are building an honest win-win relationship. If you do not ask uncomfortable (for you) questions such as 'do you really think we have a chance of doing this by October?' 'in the actual context, are we still a priority' 'what do you think could prevent us from moving forward' - and a lot more like these - you will never know where you stand and how to forecast accurately.

By being reliable, you gain reliability. By listening, you gain credibility. By being honest, you gain honesty.

Plot summary
- Forecast accuracy is essential to your investors and to manage your P&L.
- Forecast accuracy is between 95%-105% of the called number.
- A compelling event, a business reason to act is essential to define the timing in the forecast.
- You should pounder it with pipeline, best case and commit categories.

Ready, set, action!
- Do you have more than one champion? How are you activating them?
- Is your pain implicated and attached to a compelling event?
- Do you have regular touch points and multiple stakeholders to validate your progress within the opportunity?
- What are the true commit opportunities of the quarter? What actions can you take on your open opportunities to secure them?

CHAP 15: THE DATA DRIVEN COMPANY

The Dark Knight rises[36]

As you start a company, you have the undeniable competitive advantage of starting from a blank page. Nevertheless, the lack of time and resources often leads to overseeing the proper monitoring of critical data.

This means that you are driving blind and overseeing impactful data. It is more difficult for your team to identify the issues before the symptoms occur.

Alfred: 'Aren't the police supposed to be investigating them?'
Bruce Wayne/Batman: 'They don't have the tools to analyze it.'

---

[36] Photo Credit ActionVance

Alfred: 'They would if you gave them to them.'
Bruce Wayne/Batman: 'One man's tool is another man's weapon.'

The capability to redirect and rewrite your go-to-market strategy on the go and the capacity to act because of immediate notifications if something wrong occurs is crucial differentiators for your current and future investors, for yourself, and your customers.

Lucius Fox: 'The reactor is beneath the river so it could be instantly flooded in the event of a security breach.'
Miranda Tate: 'Is Bruce Wayne really that paranoid?'
Lucius Fox: 'I'm gonna plead the fifth on that one.'

--*Culture of Data & Success*--

In a data-driven company, executives save time by asking the right questions from the start and optimize their decisions by challenging external recommendations with backed up arguments, not just intuitions. However, according to a recent McKinsey Analytics survey, only 8% of companies achieve analytics at scale[37].

---

[37] https://www.mckinsey.com/business-functions/mckinsey-analytics/our-insights/breaking-away-the-secrets-to-scaling-analytics

Bruce Wayne/Batman: 'You got anything on Bane's whereabouts?'
John Blake: 'Yeah, I've got five hundred pages of tunnel records and a flashlight. I could use some help, actually.'

When the data culture is clearly defined and the information is made available, employees are aligned on a corporate mission and measure against it. Objective & Key Results[38] (OKR) become more meaningful by departments as well as globally.

Embedding data in an organization's identity, even a young one such as a startup, is not as easy as it might look. The OKRs are often a meaningful representation of the organization silos which appear when you intend to make a solution work for your analytics.

---

[38] Wikipedia: The development of OKRs is generally attributed to Andy Grove, the "Father of OKRs" *High Output Management.* OKRs comprise an objective—a clearly defined goal—and a path to achieve objectives through concrete, specific and measurable actions.

--*People, Process, Technology*--

People, process, and technology is hardly mastered at once. A tool is just a tool, and no matter how good, how easy it is to implement, it will always require:

- ☐ People for its usage and adoption.
- ☐ Proper processes to monitor and witness the benefits of its implementation.

Nevertheless, hiring operation roles implies an investment that is often overlooked. Sales operations, customer success operations, and marketing operations seem dimensioned for large corporations. Yet, a revenue operation role is critical to the success of the business, and here is why:

1. Customer-facing and marketing departments rarely have the time to properly define how to work seamlessly together, define what analytics are required and assess what tools are best suited for their needs and the company's future growth.

2. Businesspeople tend to believe that a software solution will solve all of their problems (often because they are told so by the vendors). Nevertheless, rare are the vendors who

proactively engage in deployment, adoption, and KPI monitoring conversations. The usage of the solution and return on investment are the customer's sole responsibility.

Lucius Fox: 'After your father died, Wayne Enterprises set up fourteen different defense subsidiaries. For years I've been stuttering and consolidating all the different prototypes under one roof. My roof.'
Bruce Wayne/Batman: 'Why?'
Lucius Fox: 'To keep them from falling into the wrong hands.'

3. Time is of the essence. By definition, in the startup world, businesspeople are overwhelmed with day-to-day projects. Deploying a tool that may help them is necessary but unfortunately, not essential to their day-to-day activities. Last but not least, they rarely have the skills for it.

Commissioner Gordon: 'We were in this together... then you were gone.'

Furthermore, to avoid creating deeper silos, data is not supposed to be stuck in one department. It should be shared wisely and widely across teams. To do so, centralization is essential. This could be done by someone responsible for deploying technologies, writing the proper KPIs to monitor their success and manage the process to implement. Finally, this person would be responsible for adoption. With centralization through one responsible role, there is a better understanding of how the different team works and what information and data they need to improve collectively. The company will then be data-driven and use impactful data to think and act strategically.

Alfred: 'You two should exchange notes over coffee.'

Since the revenue stream is strategic for the startup growth, it is only logical that a Revenue Operations Officer be the owner of this specific role. He/she would provide a general understanding of where your revenue could find a potential bottleneck: lack of pipeline generation, lack of conversation, increased churn, and more.

Your revenue operation officer will:

- ☐ Identify the impactful data your company requires to operate seamlessly and make impactful decisions.

- ☐ Define an adequate strategy to implement the tools required to collect, store and visualize the data.

☐ Select the best technology to deliver according to a data source, strategy, and available resources.

☐ Leverage ambassadors within each department to boost adoption and work closely with their business interests.

Bruce Wayne/Batman: 'A hero can be anyone, even a man doing something as simple and reassuring as putting a coat on a young boy's shoulders to let him know that the world hadn't ended.'

The revenue operation officer will work closely with the manager to:

☐ Define the technical requirements and optimize the correct data collection.

☐ Define the KPIs to leverage actionable insights.

☐ Ensure he/she owns the process and relay it to his/her team.

☐ Review the process regularly to improve and develop the business needs and interactions with other departments.

- Designate ambassadors/power users to relay the process and usage knowledge the operational level and adjust with field requirements to increase adoption.

Do not underestimate the task. Becoming a truly data-driven company requires a change of habits and possible change management. People must be encouraged to provide and use data, and work with others to do the same.

Plot summary
- Startups start from a blank page but are, by definition not structured enough to be data driven.
- The business departments tend to work in silos and cannot be responsible for choosing a tool, deploying it and guaranteeing its adoption.
- A central view of all the available and required data is the key to enable departments to thrive.

Ready, set, action!
- What is the most impactful data in your organization?
- How do you break silos between departments with meaningful and digestible data?
- Who has a transverse view of data linked to the revenue and can act before symptoms occur (churn, drop in pipeline generation...forecast inaccuracy)?

CHAP 16: EACH TEAM IMPACTS THE REVENUE

Jumanji: Welcome to Jungle

Everyone in your company should feel positively responsible for generating revenue. In fact, revenue should be part of the OKR[39] strategy for all teams whether they be customer-facing or R&D. This is teamwork that can only be completely shared and understood if everyone has a common goal: increase revenue.

*'A game for those who seek to find
A way to leave their world behind.'*
Jumanji: Welcome to the jungle

---

[39] Wikipedia: Andy Grove, *High Output Management*. OKRs comprise an **objective**—a clearly defined goal—and 3–5 **key results**—specific measures used to track the achievement of that goal.

Often, the combination of background, school, and continuous interactions with the same set of direct coworkers lead people to speak a different language despite their common passion: to make their startup a success. A developer has chosen to code, while a salesperson has decided to embrace into that position because of personality traits. Non-customer-facing roles and customer-facing positions may speak the same language, yet they don't understand each other business-wise.

> *'What you seek is in the basket.*
> *If you're not careful, you'll be in a casket.*
> *Trust each other, and never blink.*
> *The missing piece is not what you think.'*
>
> *Jumanji: Welcome to the jungle*

The gap[40] appears with more transparency when the opportunistic and inbound leads start to decrease, and the sales team must transition to outbound prospecting.

The marketing department is blamed for the lack of Marketing Qualified Leads (MQL) because little investment has been made with partners and networking.

---

[40] Crossing the chasm, Geoffrey A. Moore

The pipeline appears empty. Deals become scarce. Under pressure to bring revenue, the sales team bends to customers that are not in alignment with the company's value and vision. Consequently, the R&D team develops features they believe will mind the gap but don't really fit with their initial futuristic roadmap or simply stop being futuristic.

Everyone is frustrated.

Professor Shelly Oberon: 'Sometimes... it's easy to get so focused on your own stuff that... you forget other people have problems too.'

Each department blames each other when they could have a positive impact working together.

- The Product officer must review each request for enhancement thoroughly, challenging and assuring that each feature requested resolves a quantified business pain. He/she should also communicate on the vision and the roadmap both to customer-facing teams and customers.

- The marketing department can leverage champions to prepare creative content and storytelling webinars and podcasts based on business pains that the company's solution solved instead of talking about operating and operational points.

- ☐ Sales, including business development representatives, can prospect by breaking the ice with social selling, digging relevant problems at the operational level, and attaching to the executives' biggest business pains.

- ☐ Customer success can uncover new problems and business impacts at the existing customers by setting 20 to 40 business KPIs to monitor every quarter with the executive and bi-weekly basis with the users and operationals.

Dr. Smolder Bravestone: 'I can't do this!'
Moose Finbar: 'I saw you fix a helicopter in mid-air!'

When all departments converge to pulling relevant business information from their prospect and customer, the company as a whole start to act as a trusted advisor, one that can solve their business pains, the ultimate driver to find the necessary budget, and a compelling event[41] to act upon.

Dr. Smolder Bravestone: 'We can help each other. We all have special skills.'

---

[41] A compelling event must be owned by an economic buyer, defines a specific date by which a direct response to a negative business pressure must happen, it is the reason to act

Such synchronicity requires everyone to speak the same language and regularly align through an operating rhythm. It also requires key functions to be the transition between departments such as, for example:

- Customer success to be the source of testimonials stories and business KPI for marketing

- Pre-sales, to translate new features and roadmap into key-value differentiators to the sales team.

Align and execute as a team to insure the revenue climb.

'When you see an elephant begin the climb.'

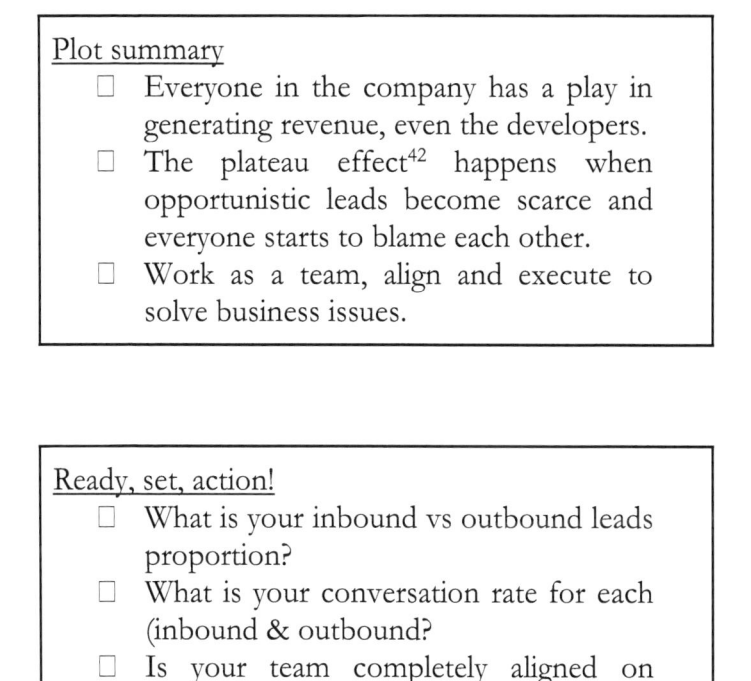

Plot summary
- Everyone in the company has a play in generating revenue, even the developers.
- The plateau effect[42] happens when opportunistic leads become scarce and everyone starts to blame each other.
- Work as a team, align and execute to solve business issues.

Ready, set, action!
- What is your inbound vs outbound leads proportion?
- What is your conversation rate for each (inbound & outbound?
- Is your team completely aligned on execution and go-to-market? Is the strategy shared?
- Does your R&D focus on features that have a business impact on your prospects and customers? Are they aware?

---

[42] Crossing the Chasm. Geoffrey A Moore.

CHAP 17: MEDDIC AS A COMMON LANGUAGE

In the year 2015, I joined Sprinklr. I had the chance to spend time with Dick Dunkel, who ran onboarding and sales enablement at the time. Dick was one of the founders of MEDDIC[44] during his time at PTC.

At the time, the PTC team's intentions were to transform their success from unconsciously competent to consciously competent, repeating the reasons for their achievements consistently, mastering a complete execution in delivering the numbers and the forecast accuracy.[45]

---

[43] Photo by Dmitry Ratushny
[44] To read more about MEDDIC/MEDDICC, read MEDDICC by Andy Whyte with foreword from Dick Dunkel and Jack Napoli.
[45] This Chapter is a quick introduction to MEDDIC to know more read MEDDIC by Andy Whyte.

Nowadays, MEDDIC has spread globally to many large corporations and startups (MongoDB, Snowflake, Datadog, Medallia, Sprinklr, and more). However, as the acronym spread its wings, many have implemented it poorly, missing out on each word's essential understandings.

In my humble opinion, MEDDIC is not one methodology as many may call it. It is a checklist, a diagnostic tool that combines many more essential methodologies such as the Challenger Sale, Value Selling, Spin Selling, Sandler Selling, Customer-Centric Selling, and more. Anyone that tells you MEDDIC is 'their' methodology has it all wrong.

MEDDIC is, in fact, a repository of best-in-class methodologies.

Furthermore, I personally believe that MEDDIC can serve as a common language to the company's different departments. It should not be taught or used by sales and management, nor should it be a simple gatekeeper in your CRM. It should be a tool to accelerate communication between departments to maximize your customer experience and revenue.

'Widespread support for a supplier across their team is the number one thing senior decision makers look for in making a purchase decision.' - The challenger sale[46]

---

[46] Book reference: The challenger sale by Brent Adamson and Matthew Dixon

Successful organizations rely upon a group of diverse people with distinct skill sets. Each person owns his/her own role in making the company a functioning whole.

One person alone is not meant to manage R&D, Sales, Marketing, and Customer Success. As the startup scales, so does each department, creating inherent cracks in the overall company communication. The following definitions should highlight how you may choose to use MEDDIC in your organization to simplify some simple cross-team communication.

Note: other benefits of using MEDDIC include better forecast accuracy, pipeline creation (high ACV), shortened sales cycle, and customer satisfaction.

MEDDIC stands for the following: Metrics, Economic Buyer, Decision Process, Decision Criteria, Implicate the pain and Champions.

--*Metrics*--

If you are educating a market, chances are your prospects have no idea of how to measure themselves on the topic you address. Assist your prospect in building a set of meaningful Key Performance Indicators relevant to their business. The more data you collect - and by data, I mean meaningful data... not asking your prospect for the number of servers or users, information that is only relevant to you - the more pertinent you will be. Developing a conversation and deep-dive workshops around Key performance indicators (KPIs) matching their corporate objective and business strategies will secure your position for renewal and provide deep insights into the business impacts of their functional problems and how you can feel the gap.

'What if customers' greatest need is to figure out exactly what they need?' -The challenger sale

Common language note

Bring your customer success people early on in a sales campaign. They can reassure your prospect, give them perspective, and enable you to go further into the metrics uncovering.

--Economic Buyer--

The economic buyer is often perceived as the person whom you must meet to make the deal happen. In reality, if well-identified, he or she is sometimes so far off, you may never directly meet him/her. You can, however, get the deal done.

The economic buyer is the person that, if he or she says yes, no one else can say no. More importantly, he or she sees an economic benefit (increase revenue, reduce cost, reduce risk) in investing in your solution. An economic buyer can be reached indirectly via your champions[47].

'What sets the best suppliers apart is not the quality of their products, but the value of their insight—new ideas to help customers either make money or save money in ways they didn't even know were possible.' - The challenger sale

Common language note

Align your documents and proposals with C-level perspective so that your prospect and economic buyer receives a transparent, straightforward, and understandable value proposition. Use your revenue operation officer, C-levels, founders to assist in crafting such documents with the proper insights (metrics/pains).

---

[47] Refer to Chap 6: No champ, no deal.

--Decision Criteria--

The decision criteria are yours. You must influence them from the moment you do your segmentation, from the first meeting. The price, for example, should never be decision criteria. If it comes to this. You have failed. If your prospect is hurting and requires a solution, they will go for the best, not the cheapest.

There is an alignment between your differentiators and their needs. The decision is often more complex than just a technical evaluation. Your understanding of their issues, your expertise, and your positioning to answer the problems, your vision, your story, and your people are entirely relevant. Document their decision criteria and ensure your teams remain in alignment after signing the deal to extend and prolong your relationship. Furthermore, R&D can benefit from getting a clear view of the strengths and weaknesses of the field.

Common language note

Your customer should receive a seamless experience from sales to deployment to customer success. Listing properly the decision criteria validating them with the customer regularly and organizing R&D discussion is gratifying for both the vendor and the customer.

--Decision Process--

It takes a village to get a deal done. No sales can do it alone. Mastering the decision process in its granularity is essential. The process is a moving target. It changes at all times. Some new companies have renamed MEDDIC in MEDDPIC. In my humble opinion, this could be a mistake. If you hire young and junior sales, it might lead your organization in the wrong direction; the paper process is often let to the end. By working it early with the customer as part of his decision process, understanding the impact of legal review and security from the earliest conversation enables true execution.

Common language note

Giving clear visibility to the departments - finance, legal, security, and more - enhances productivity and transparency and avoids frustrations from all parts.

--Implicate the pain--

Proceed with caution. The I in MEDDIC does not refer to 'identify the pain' as some may claim but 'implicate the pain'. Your prospect will not engage with you if you tell him/her what is wrong.

If you tell someone they are doing it wrong, they probably will not listen[48]. If you listen and have them tell you what's wrong, if they verbalize their issues, you can assist them with your expertise in solving their pains. No customer will give you money just because you are shiny and bright. No. You must respond to some issues rooted in their business operations by either reducing cost, increasing revenue, or reducing their risk of exposure. (for more on this, read Spin and Sandler selling)

Common language note

Without a good understanding of the customer pain points' business implications, explained by them -implicated- and not identified & assumed by yourself, your delivery people cannot do a good job in the implementation phase. Your customer success team will be bound to fail, and your renewal team will never know why ... the customer has churned[49].

---

[48] Spin selling by Neil Rackham, Asking questions the Sandler way by Antonio Garrido
[49] Refer to Chap 18: The 0% Churn Objective

--*Champion (s)*[50]--

First of all, the more...the merrier! He (or she) has a personal interest in working with you. Whether driven by fear or ambition, your champion will sell on your behalf within the company when you are not there. Champions are essential in a vendor/customer relationship.

Common language note

Your pre-sales and SDRs team can develop their own champions and strengthen your position. To continue with a seamless experience, your customer success should maintain a similar relationship with your champion, which will favor adoption. Last, champions are the bread and butter of your marketing department, they constitute the essence of your webinars, events, and testimonials. The notion and definition of a champion must be commonly shared across the different roles of the organization.

Practice and practice again, whether you decide to use MEDDIC or something else as a common language. Implement, execute, and ensure adoption. Never stop using it, as soon as you stop the revenue communication flow between all departments, the threat is back on again.

---

[50] Refer to Chap 6: No champ, no deal.

Plot summary
- ☐ MEDDIC is an acronym that serves as a diagnostic and checklist in your sales campaigns.
- ☐ MEDDIC can be a language shared between the different departments to enhance productivity.
- ☐ MEDDIC is a repository of many other sales methodologies.
- ☐ The I in MEDDIC is not about identifying the pain but implicating the pain.

Ready, set, action!
- ☐ How control do you have over your forecast?
- ☐ Who, besides your sales team, has a clear understanding of the sales campaigns?
- ☐ How involved and creative are non-sales departments to solving roadblocks and issues with a prospect?
- ☐ Does your R&D understand what a pain is and what a business pain can represent for their roadmap?

CHAP 18: 0% CHURN OBJECTIVE

Pulp Fiction[51]

Churn is overlooked. Churn is overseen. It is the KPI you wish to turn your back on, the one you wish didn't exist. Yet, it stands, haunting you. Its rate, when high, stands as a reminder of your process failure. Much like Pulp Fiction, Churn can teach you a lot about your company and who you are... Will you ignore it?

Jules Winnfield: 'Look, do you wanna play blind man? Go walk with the shepherd. But me, my eyes are wide fucking open.'

In 2005, under Marc Benioff's guidance, Salesforce was approaching a $2B market cap. Simultaneously however, the company was experiencing a high churn rate. Despite its undeniable success in the CRM space, Salesforce struggled under the weight of its

---

[51] Photo by amirali mirhashemian on Unsplash

customer churn – until it addressed the matter with all its might.

Will you address the matter of churn with all your energy and will?

A company close to my heart, Sprinklr, holds one of the following values: 'Fix it, don't complain.' And it isn't just a value. Ragy Thomas, CEO of Sprinklr, reviews all customers at risk of churn weekly and puts a plan in motion with the constant objective of a 0% churn rate. How often do you monitor your churn rate? How often do you even discuss the risk, before a renewal fails to materialise?

Marsellus Wallace: 'Fuck pride. Pride only hurts, it never helps.'

I, unfortunately, had the chance to sit on those Monday calls personally. If I were on it, it meant that one of my customers was at risk. I did not want to be on those calls. Nobody did. Especially when you had to report bad news to your CEO.

A CEO's involvement in fixing churn is more than essential. It is a question of survival. Churn is not only hurting revenue. It is hurting your future sales and your reputation. Ragy mentioned it at the WebSummit in Lisbon in 2018: 'Acquisition and churn go hand in hand. Otherwise, you are trying to fill a bucket that is leaking'.

Ask questions, understand the situation; don't just get comfortable with answers you wish to hear, get to the bottom of the problem and challenge your teams. Where does the issue come from? The idea is not to find someone to blame – but to find the people who can fix it. Find out where and how to act, who to mandate, and who to delegate to for the best impact.

Jules Winnfield: 'If my answers frighten you, then you should cease asking scary questions.'

So, what are the origins of the churn? Usually, its causes fall into one of these four categories:

#1: Business model issues:

You've been searching yourself; you have changed your positioning and pricing model one too many times. You've sold too low, you've sold too small, you've sold to immature companies that had no resources to implement nor see the value of your solution. In other words, you've rushed through getting an order form without foreseeing a long-term relationship.

#2: Stakeholder issues:

You've identified and implicated the pain; you've laid out your value, you've implemented well-with a super user admin. You've bet on one person alone. You've forgotten to multiply the stakeholders. No one else knows your value. As soon as this person moves position and is replaced, so might your solution.

#3: Product issues:

Your product might have faults - or it might not fit with the way your customer operates. Sometimes, things simply don't deliver their expected value. Beware of selling a roadmap,and take care with how you sell it. Make sure your customer knows the details of the features delivery schedule to avoid disappointment. Bugs and delays can generate frustrations. Is your customer being treated with empathy? How long has he or she been paying without using the solution? What have been the business impacts for them?

#4: Executive alignment issue:

No one on your side or their side has aligned on business KPIs to monitor quarterly. You've let your admin people and their operational people do the job and expect great results; leadership must be involved. Perhaps this category reflects your organization working in silos, proving misalignment between Sales, Pre-Sales, Delivery & Customer Success.

This is a non-exhaustive list. But, now that you know some of the main reasons, you can address them to avoid finding yourself in a high churn rate situation. If the damage has already been done, however, consider the following solutions:

Jules Winnfield: 'And that's what we're gonna be. We're gonna be cool. Now, Ringo, I'm gonna count to three.'

Speak up:

Encourage your team to speak up as soon as they identify risk of churn. Give them a framework – to avoid a weekly rat race). Create a risk assessment framework that your customer-facing team must fill out: why do they believe there is a risk? Have they identified the origin? What is the overall impact on the customer? Who is involved? Have they measured it? Who at your company is involved in fixing the matter? What resources do they need to fix it?

Mia Wallace: 'Uncomfortable silences. Why do we feel it's necessary to yak about bullshit to be comfortable?'

Time is your greatest asset:

If you find yourself facing potential churn, you've screwed up. And that's ok. Whether it's just because of you or because of your whole team, it doesn't matter. If you've watched Pulp Fiction, you'll know that each character has a chance to redeem themselves. If your customer gives you that chance, you might just be able to redeem yourself. But only if you're sufficiently humble. Please take the chance to do so it's a test you need to pass.

The Wolf: 'You must be Jules, which would make you Vincent. Let's get down to brass tacks, gentlemen. If I was informed correctly, the clock is ticking, is that right, Jimmie?'

Redemption:

If you face yourself with a situation of potential churn, you've screwed up - and that's OK-. Individually or as a team, it does not matter. If you've watched Pulp Fiction, you'll know that each character has a chance to redeem themselves. If your customer is giving you a chance, you might find yourself fortunate to redeem yourself. Be humble. Take the chance to do so. It's a test you need to pass.

Vincent Vega: 'Did you ever hear the philosophy that once a man admits that he's wrong, he is immediately forgiven for all wrongdoings?'

Do what's right:

In fact, go above and beyond. That's what your customers deserve from paying you and trusting you. Some customers cannot be saved. Let them be, let them go, do not lock them if they cannot be successful. In the long term, selflessness and righteousness pay off, always. Do the right thing.

Vincent Vega: 'It's the little differences. I mean they got the same shit over there that they got here, but it's just — it's just there it's a little different.'

Plot summary
- ☐ Your churn rate can tell you a lot about your company and who you are, will you ignore it?
- ☐ There are 4 main categories for the churn: Business model issues, stakeholders' issues, product issues and exec alignment issues.
- ☐ Speak up, act early, find redemption and do the right thing are important.

Ready, set, action!
- ☐ How often do you monitor your churn rate?
- ☐ How often do you discuss the risk with your customer facing teams?
- ☐ Who is involved? How much of the executive team participates in managing the churn?
- ☐ Are you satisfied with the number of stakeholders involved at each of your customers? How often do you meet with your customers' executive team?

BOOK III

SCALE IT UP

CHAP 19: THE SDR[52] VALUE

Ghostbusters[53]

Sales development representatives (SDRs), also called BDRs (Business Development Representative) or my personal favorite ADRs (Account Development Representative), are the frontlines of your company, your solution, and, more importantly, your value. They are your prospects' first impression.

Peter Venkman: '24 hours a day, seven days a week. No job is too big. No fee is too big.'

SDRs are to be treated respectfully, coached, developed, and handed leads with utmost consideration – especially when it comes to the most dangerous category: the inbound leads. In the specific

---

[52] SDR: sales development representatives, also called BDR, ADR are often asked to schedule meetings for account executives
[53] Photo credit Andrew Martin

case of an inbound lead, the prospect has done some research; their mind is made up. They may even have talked to some of your competitors and developed an idea of their budget and pricing. This is dangerous because your field of influence is reduced. You have to use all your skills and techniques to reset the situation in the discovery phase and 'differentiate' yourself.

Ray Stantz: 'Drop everything, Venkman. We got one.'

SDRs are, by definition, juniors in their sales experience. Those who are particularly talented tend to learn quickly and are driven by an ambition for other positions such as SDR manager, inside sales, account executives…

This is why you want to dedicate time and attention to choosing the right person. You want people with drive and natural curiosity – people who have the will and skills to become thoughtful detectives and experts in their field.

Janine Melnitz: 'Do you believe in UFOs, astral projections, mental telepathy, ESP, clairvoyance, spirit photography, telekinetic movement, full trance mediums, the Loch Ness monster, and the theory of Atlantis?'
Winston Zeddmore: 'If there's a steady paycheck in it, I'll believe in anything you say.'

No one is going to argue with the fact that outbound leads are the toughest to get, and thus, the most rewarding.

Peter Venkman: 'Spengler, are you serious about actually catching a ghost?'
Egon Spengler: 'I'm always serious.'

So, when someone responds to an email positively, you may feel like you've just won a brand new ECTO 1959 Cadillac. Except if, from the very beginning, you were haunting the right manor, with the right bait and the adequate materials.

Raymond Stantz: 'You know, it's just occurred to me we really haven't had a completely successful test of this equipment.'

To do so, they must have quality objectives. Unfortunately, when it comes to measuring SDRs, the most common KPIs are: 'meeting scheduled', 'number of calls', 'number of emails,' and so on. Worst, in some cases, SDRs are asked to provide a budget, the name of the decision-maker, and a time to close a deal after... just one or two interactions. How do you think your prospects feel when asked how much budget he has for a solution he does not know about… or if he is the decision maker?

Egon Spengler: 'Don't cross the streams.'
Peter Venkman: 'Why?'
Egon Spengler: 'It would be bad.'
Peter Venkman: 'I'm fuzzy on the whole good/bad thing. What do you mean, 'bad'?'
Egon Spengler: 'Try to imagine all life as you know it stopping instantaneously and every molecule in your body exploding at the speed of light.'
Raymond Stantz: 'Total protonic reversal.'

Peter Venkman: 'Right. That's bad. Okay. Alright, important safety tip. Thanks Egon.'

SDRs should work with the account executives who offer them a path to success and 'business strategies' vision of the prospects – those who know how to work with their team to positively impact both at the operational and executive levels. By working together on a defined path, the SDRs and account executives can ask complementary questions relevant and pertinent to the prospect.

Peter Venkman: 'I love this plan! I'm excited to be a part of it! Let's do it!'

Last but not least, mindset is everything. Train your SDRs, give them content that allows them to differentiate themselves, align their objectives with their peers, and teach them social selling. Their position can be crucial in the generation revenue chain. Make it so.

Winston Zeddmore: 'Ray, when someone asks you if you're a god, you say "YES"!'

> Plot summary
> - SDRs are the front line, your company's first impression, they must be coached and developed.
> - Value Quality over Quantity.
> - No results can be achieved without understanding the segmentation, and teamwork.

> Ready, set, action!
> - How do you currently compensate your SDRs?
> - How do you recruit your SDRs?
> - Do you see them as the frontline getting meetings and touch points or do you help them develop in their role and grow?
> - What is your SDRs retention plan?
> - How can you help your team work together to divide and conquer on opportunities?

CHAP 20: SALES PROCESS IN THE SUBSCRIPTION ERA

Mary Poppins[54]

When the time comes to put a sales process in place, CRMs often carry a laid-out process that only requires slight customization. You can tweak it and improve it, but, as it is, it will remain a sales approach. It often starts a lead and ends with a contract.

---

[54] Photo by Taylor Wright

The process is linear, straightforward and often looks like this:

1.Lead:
Interest from a prospect to engage in a discussion.

2. Discovery:
Understanding of the situation and implications.

3. Evaluation:
Definition whether your company can provide a solution to fix the issue.

4. Technical Go/No-Go:
Validation of your company solution as the best choice.

5. Proposal:
Sized and budgeted scenarios based on the phases 2, 3 and 4.

6. Negotiation:
Best win-win proposal including final legal 'parked' review, payment terms, length of contract and price.

7. Close:
All paperwork validated to proceed for booking.

Bert/Mr. Dawes Sr: 'Winds in the east, there's a mist coming in, like something is brewing, about to begin.'

In this new decade, more than ever, the standard for many industries is a subscription and renewal model.

Even in a tacit renewal situation, your customer has a choice to renew or leave you after his initial engagement, typically after 12 months.

Mary Poppins: 'That's a pie-crust promise; easily made, easily broken!'

The risk of churn[55] is much like the Damocles sword. Putting a customer cycle in place, including the overlap of essential roles instead a linear sales process might reduce this risk.

--*Lead & Discovery*--

The Sales Development Representative (SDR) and Account Executive should team up for any prospecting and outbound activity:

Benefits for the company: The Account Executive brings the segmentation expertise: why are we targeting these accounts in priority? What business strategies in the prospect's annual report align with our value proposal? What could we do to solve its problems?

Onboard with this messaging, the SDR will uncover critical and decisive information at an operational level. The SDR should help prepare and attend manager-level meetings to leverage additional stakeholders' information, thus growing the opportunity.

---

[55] Refer to chap 18: 0% churn objective

Benefits for the customer: complete alignment in the outbound messaging, feel recognized as an individual, not part of mass mailing. Can benefit from an open conversation with experts who understand his/her issue.

Customer Cycle: upsell and cross-sell are repeating this new phase even with existing costumes. In this case, the cycle should be worked from then on as a Trio SDR- Account Executive- Customer Success.

Mrs. Banks: 'As a matter of fact, since you hired Mary Poppins, the most extraordinary things seem to have come over the household.'
Mr. Banks: 'Is that so?'
Mrs. Banks: 'Take Ellen, for instance. She hasn't broken a dish all morning.'
Mr. Banks: 'Really? Well, that is extraordinary.'

--Evaluation - Technical Go/No Go--

At this stage, the SDR and Account Executive have understood the problems they can solve. Ideally, the prospect has shared a clear outline of what the 3 whys[56] will become.

During this phase, the Account Executive should work hand in hand with a pre-sales engineer through workshops. The purpose of multiplying touchpoints through these is to identify use cases, potential

---

[56] Why do something, why do it with your solution, why do it now: refer to chap 14: forecast accuracy

technical and security roadblocks, and prepare for an executive presentation.

Customer Cycle: If this is an existing customer, the working pair will become a trio, with a member of the customer success staff bringing proof points from other existing projects and key leading indicators to ensure upsell/cross-sell.

Mary Poppins: 'In every job that must be done, there is an element of fun. You find the fun, and the job's a game!'

--Proposal--

The proposal comes once there is a verbal agreement, a technical validation ideally confirmed by the mention of 'vendor of choice' or 'entering exclusive negotiations'.
The Account Executive usually leads this part, occasionally supported by his direct manager. This is, in my humble opinion, a mistake. Even for a 'new logo,' it is crucial to show a united front at the moment of the proposal.

Bringing the deployment or Services team and a customer success representative to the table reassures the prospect and clarifies the contract signature process. It proves expertise and ensures all teams are in alignment so that no surprises or disappointments shall emerge after the deal is done.

Besides, most proposals should include the customer success renewal fee and potentially additional one-time service fees. These fees will be better perceived and associated with value when presented by the people who will deliver them. After all, people buy from people, and providing expertise can only add value at the proposal moment.

Mary Poppins: 'A spoonful of sugar helps the medicine go down.'

--Negotiation[57] --

Again, a negotiation should start as a united front for a very particular reason: the person in the room holding the most information usually wins the negotiation.
It is no surprise that, due to their lack of experience, startups drag this phase. As a united front, with crucial information found at operational (SDR), technical and security (pre-sales), and user (customer success) level, a negotiation can be held with a full picture of the situation.

What is the prospective customer going through? And:

1. Why do they need to act?
2. Why with your startup specifically?
3. Why now rather than in six months?

Bert: 'What did I tell ya? There's the whole world at your feet.'

---

[57] Refer to chap 13: Negotiation skills

--Win – Deployment- Cruising--

After the negotiation should come the win, the customer's celebrations, an onboarding process, a deployment, and a cruising phase.

During these phases, the Deployment and Customer Success teams will lead the way. This new overlap in their roles may reveal new pains, new champions, and new use cases in this new cycle. Referrals and testimonials will allow for constant growth. Here, the SDR, Pre-Sales team, and Account Executive should remain involved at all times.

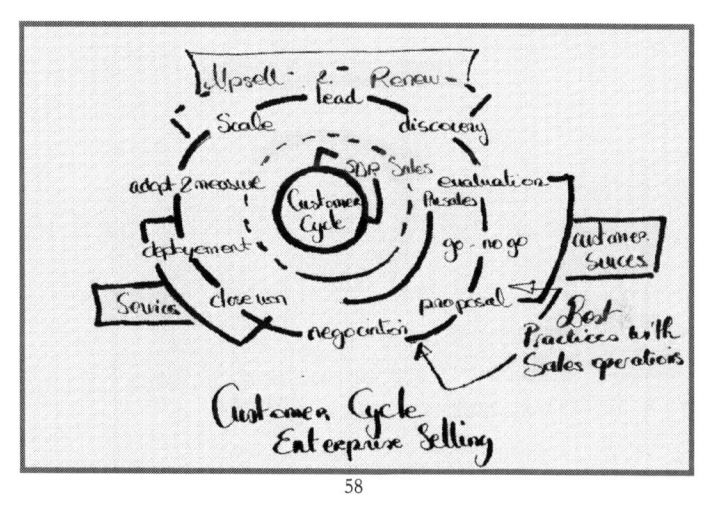

![Customer Cycle Enterprise Selling whiteboard diagram][58]

This organized Cycle process and overlap of roles offers direct benefits such as reducing the silos

---

[58] Whiteboarding extract of conversation with actual clients on how to optimize customer facing roles to serve the customer better.

between the customer-facing roles and smooth customer experience.

Bert: 'Mary Poppins, practically perfect in every way.'

Plot summary
- ☐ Customer experience should drive your sales process.
- ☐ Your process should not be linear in a renewal business model.
- ☐ Overlap of the teams is important for a seamless customer experience.

Ready, set, action!
- ☐ Are your sales representatives leveraging all other teams? How?
- ☐ Do you currently have a great knowledge of the Business KPIs you have an impact on?
- ☐ How can your customers feel more engaged before the customer signs? What is their area of expertise? How can you leverage it?

CHAP 21: TARGET AND ACHIEVE COMPLEX DEALS

Jaws: 'We're gonna need a bigger boat'

When a startup decides to go after the big deals, the complex ones, the ones with a sales cycle of 6 to 18 months and multiple departments involved, we commonly call this stage, in the sales jargon, 'the enterprise.'

Which, come to think of it, is a big deal, as big as a great white shark. How do you transform from catching the small fry to a great white?

'There has never been an adventure thriller quite as terrifying, yet enjoyable as 'jaws'.'
– Gary Arnold, The Washington Post

CEOs who were comfortably growing revenue opportunistically by closing small deals with the Small and Medium Business (SMB) market might tell you the same thing as Gary Arnold. Why? Because of the bigger fish's exhilarating potential: bringing in the regular six figure deals and a significant number of seven figure deals. It is, indeed, terrifying yet enjoyable.

Why is it terrifying?

First, it requires a transformation at all levels even for a young startup. Are all the people cut out for large 'enterprise' deals? Does the marketing, R&D, and Sales align with the longer-term vision? After all, when you have been working a certain way for the last three to four years, and it has worked, why, oh why change everything?

Chief Brody: 'I can do anything. I am the chief of police.'

That's what a CEO might think but never dare to say, with reason. To make the project successful, the CEO will want to rally the troops, focus on adoption. Unfortunately, people, in general, are reluctant to change, even in the startup world.

Hooper: 'I think I'm familiar with the fact that you are going to ignore this particular problem until it swims up and bites you in the ass.'

So how do you make the transformation happen and how do you get people to adopt your new enterprise sales strategy?

The first thing you will have to do is to align all your head of departments:

- Marketing will have to reduce low level/mass growth hacking to focus on quality high-end events to access C-levels.

- R&D will need to define a long-term roadmap; A large enterprise vision cut out for Fortune 500 executives.

- Delivery will need to staff up either internally or externally, partnering with integrators. Larger and complex deals may imply additional services.

Denherder: 'Is that $3,000 bounty on the shark in cash or check?'

The next thing you will have to deal with is sales:

- Review who has the skills and drive to move up the ladder.

- Train them to act as trusted advisors and slowly move away from transactional deals to long term and visionary deals.

- ☐ Assist them move away from the feature/function's conversation to a problem-solving conversation

- ☐ Hire additional senior salespeople who have experience to lead the way.

Note: you may need to change the compensation plan to support the changes and keep a high level of motivation.

The one thing you want to avoid is bad recruitment. Buying a superstar who has closed multi-million-dollar deals may end up a terrible investment if his or her personality is not cut out for teamwork with millennials. You want to create adoption. Therefore, anyone senior you hire must have experience in the startup world. Don't hire the lone wolf.[59]

Quint: 'Don't need any two-bit chaperones to tag along. By myself, alone, just me and that great white. 10 quid, and I'll bring ya the head, the tail and everything between, the whole damn fish!'

Any type of transformation represents a delicate moment in a company's life, whether it be within a startup or a large corporation. Here are a few additional tips to consider:

---

[59]Refer to Chap 22&23

- ☐ Don't try to do it in 3 months. Your average size deal will not go from 25K to 150K in such a short timeframe. It will only add unnecessary pressure.

- ☐ Communicate weekly about all the changes you are going to make.

- ☐ Train your people regularly on the change of messaging.

- ☐ Focus on adoption and be firm with anyone who is not ready to support your strategy.

Mayor Vaughn: 'Martin, it's all psychological. You yell, Barracuda, everybody says, huh, what? You yell Shark, we've got a panic on our hands-on the Fourth of July.'

Last but not least, preparation is essential for any well-executed plan, prepare who, what, and when well ahead of launch and communicate accordingly.

> Plot summary
> - ☐ Targeting complex deals requires organization, segmentation and the right people.
> - ☐ Moving from opportunistic SMB to Enterprise is a transformation, even for the startup.
> - ☐ Marketing, Delivery and R&D must be involved and engaged in the transformation.
> - ☐ A well-executed plan is a well thought plan. Prepare everything, communicate well, train and assess regularly.

> Ready, set, action!
> - ☐ Assess your people: does your team have the skill and will to take on the complex deals?
> - ☐ Assess your strategy: are you completely aligned with marketing and R&D? Is your segmentation matching?
> - ☐ Assess your plan, is it clear and actionable? Who is challenging the transformation and why?

CHAP 22: FIGHT THE COMPETITION

Die Hard[60]

There are several types of competitions, by nature, you should always see it coming, yet down the line of your startup life, you might be taken by surprise. Let's analyze the consequences of an unsettling yet organized competitor disrupting your plans.

---

[60] Photo by Brandon Erlinger-Ford

With less resources, you can still turn things around, much like John McClane at the top of the Nakatomi Tower.

Sizing the momentum is everything

You did not see it coming, you were cruising and then suddenly, a lesser solution, a product that you did not even consider worthy of your attention is attacking your market directly.

Dispatcher: 'Attention, whoever you are; this channel is reserved for emergency calls only.'
John McClane: 'No fucking shit lady, does it sound like I'm ordering a pizza?'

Maybe a competitor came up using aggressive prices or with functionality similar to yours. Perhaps a large corporation has bought another startup. One that you did not even bother considering your direct competition but, with fresh money, R&D resources, and an army of salespeople, is now quite worthy of your attention.

John McClane : '[after McClane sets off massive explosion] Is the building on fire?'
Sergeant Al Powell : 'No, but it's gonna need a paint job and a shit load of screen doors.'

Differentiators and lifetime expectancy

Fighting a competitor is stimulating, it is better than fighting alone for the education of a market. If your competitors have caught up on your unique differentiators, take it as a good sign, they are your copycat!

Why are copycats good?

They push you to consistently innovate. Your unique differentiators have a lifetime expectancy and copycats put a rhythm to your vision.

They validate your total addressable market (TAM) and the direction you have given to your product and services.

They assist you in educating the market, opening prospects eyes on problems they have not identified yet, or identified incorrectly. They open the door so you can compete with your value and expertise.

John McClane: 'Welcome to the party pal!'

This is not a drill: prove your execution skills

Start by identifying the strengths and weaknesses of your competitor. Why didn't you see it coming? What is their profile? Who are they targeting? How do they operate?

John McClane : 'These guys are mostly European judging by their clothing labels and... [long pause] cigarettes. They're well-financed and very slick. [...] Add all that up, I don't know what the fuck it means, but you got some bad-ass perpetrators and they're here to stay.'

Dedicate a war room and a squad team to the subject matter. If you want to eliminate a competition that has caught you unaware, you must revise your own positioning. Why are you at risk? How, why and when the market has been shifting?

Hans Gruber : 'Do you really think you have a chance against us, Mr. Cowboy?'

It is time to break silos, and it is a good pressure exercise for your executive team. Personalities usually show their true nature under pressure. You may be surprised by people's reaction and possibly, their egos rising.

Know that you may even lose exceptional talent under such circumstances, fear can take some and raise others. That's ok, if one is not part of your united front in times of difficulties, then little value will come out of that person in the long run.

John McClane : 'Now, you listen to me, jerk-off, if you're not a part of the solution, you're a part of the problem. Quit being a part of the fucking problem and put the other guy back on!'

Craft your plan. Focus on:

- Caring for your existing customers. If you are not doing so already, ensure your customers are well taken care of – with no complaints, and a high NPS score. Make personal calls from C-level executives to C-level executives, show them confidence, and reassure them by providing a long-term vision. Anchor them back to the reasons why they chose you in the first place.

- Securing your ongoing prospect with a value-added understanding of their problems. Make sure to provide value at every step of your sales process. Understand the problems you are solving. Attach your product and your expertise to the global solution you are providing.

- Bringing your long-term vision closer in the timeline to differentiate. This is the moment for your R&D people to reorganize the roadmap and deliver quickly on USPs.

Keep in mind that new features may look good on the product but will not help you win or upsell customers if they have no business impact.

It is time to be unpredictable and shake your competition's perspective by delivering on your vision.

Hans Gruber: 'We do NOT alter the plan!'
Karl: 'And, if HE alters it?'

To win the war you'll need allies

The best form of defense is to attack. Attack with all your might and, more importantly, with your most powerful weapon: your existing customers and champions.

If you were not leveraging them before, now is the time. Your long-term customers will assist you in neutralizing your opponent.

Sergeant Al Powell : 'You know we got a pool going on you.'
John McClane : 'What kind of odds am I getting?'

You may be surprised by how valuable your customers are. They can give you insights on what your competitor is trying to achieve. They can speak up on your behalf to your current prospect. They also may wish to participate in building a valuable and business impactful roadmap.

Argyle : [Argyle shuts the limo door] If this is their idea of Christmas, I *gotta* be here for New Year's.

Plot summary

Whether your competitor takes you by surprise or you had seen it coming, the steps are easy to follow (die hard spoiler included):

☐ Do not panic *and make sure you wear shoes*

☐ Assess your competition *even if it implies writing their names on your arm.*

☐ Work your differentiators *and keep the detonators at all times.*

☐ Choose your allies carefully *and do not rely on the FBI.*

☐ Put a plan in motion *and scream Yippee Ki Yay Motherfucker.*

Ready, set, action!
  ☐ How prepared are you to attack?
  ☐ How much visibility do you have on your future USPs? How much visibility have you given to your most trusted customers?
  ☐ Do you know who your allies are?

CHAP 23: THE ART OF THE COMPENSATION PLAN

Gremlins

Managing sales for non-sales founders is a bit of a nightmare. This is why it is important to stop and analyze the consequences of a sales team's rising within the company culture, so you don't end up feeding the bad sales after midnight.

It's the startup's life. The founders do the prospecting and close their first customer by themselves. When it is time to hire their first salespeople, they do so while remaining quite involved in the sales campaigns, sometimes even too much.

They justify it because they own the tribal knowledge, the company's story, the passion for their solution, the vision for the future, and the problems they have solved for their existing customers.

This can work on the short term, especially when hiring junior sales. However, soon enough, founders can no longer sustain their rhythm, particularly when an additional round of investments requires their attention. It is time for a proper sales delegation.

As Gizmo would say: *'uh oh';* here comes trouble.

Acquiring a sales team can be as tricky as setting your pricing strategy. You must select the right talents and ensure you set them for success.

To do so; you must first unload all of the tribal knowledge in a structured, easy to read and easy to digest consultative document also commonly referred to as Playbook or Value Framework.

This company bible will be used by all and be especially valuable to your customer-facing teams.
Your playbook/value framework/company bible is something quite difficult to achieve on your own. You will soon notice that external help is useful for collecting opinions, confronting the inconsistencies, and challenging your comfort zone. This document should be your company's quintessence delivered in an easy-to-digest, absorb, and consult format. It should collect at a **minimum** the following:

☐ Your USPs (Unique Selling Proposition): the features you provide that are unique to your company and that no one else has on the market. Features that have a tremendous positive business impact on your customers.

☐ The personas you address, their collective pains, and negative business impact.

☐ Your success stories and use cases are backed up with metrics or business KPIs.

The playbook accelerates the onboarding of your recruits and ensures that in their responsibility of being in a customer-facing role, they maximize your value, your reputation, and your customer engagement at all times.

Grandfather: 'With Mogwai comes much responsibility. I cannot sell him at any price.'

Nevertheless, a playbook, a value framework or a company bible does not set the tone for ground rules. If a deal closes and looks shady, if there was ever a side letter, a verbal promise, or even a discount that was not too aggressive, you have a sales issue on your plate and ...a Gremlin in the house.

Rand Peltzer: 'So if your air conditioner goes on the fritz or your washing machine blows up, or your video recorder conks out before you call the repairman, turn on all the lights, check all the closets and cupboards, look under all the beds, 'cause you never can tell. There just might be a gremlin in your house.'

Set rules and gatekeeping steps to avoid proposals being sent before approval and thorough brainstorming. Set a checklist of documents and requirements to be socialized with your customers. Provide an internal checklist of requirements for booking guidance.

Chinese Boy: 'Look, Mister, there are some rules that you've got to follow.'

Review the compensation plan and warrant that the commissions are based on revenue, discount level, margin valorization, product mix, and long-term strategy.

Billy: 'Yeah, what kind of rules?'

1. No discount levels without formal approbation: you can also teach your sales to create value scenarios where the customer can choose the size of the deal not based on discount but a value for budget drawer quote.

2. No side letters of any kind, no promises, verbal or by email (especially future features and roadmap estimate). Anything that must be committed should be part of a formal agreement and approved by your executive team in writing.

3. Avoid short-term contracts, POC, and pilots at all costs. They drive away resources from engaged paying customers.

Chinese Boy: '(..) But the most important rule, the rule you can never forget, no matter how much he cries, no matter how much he begs, never feed him after midnight.'

Instead, reward positive behavior:

- ☐ If a customer has agreed to engage for three years instead of the typical twelve months, do pay commissions for the additional years.

- ☐ If a salesperson has maximized the value of a deal by selling additional expertise, thus securing the project's success, don't undermine the commission of such services vs. license.

- ☐ If a salesperson has developed and turned a customer into a lifetime champion that serves public testimonials, interviews, and webinars, do reward your salesperson too.

- ☐ Last but not least, do reward forecast accuracy. If you find salespeople who create pipeline consistently and forecast accurately, it is as golden as the size of deals they bring in.

'Perhaps someday, you will be ready. Until then, Mogwai waits.'

Plot summary
- ☐ Unload all of the tribal knowledge in a structured, easy to read and easy to digest consultative document (Playbook).
- ☐ Set some ground rules and gatekeeping steps to avoid proposals being sent before approval or thorough brainstorming.
- ☐ Set compensation plan not only on revenue but also discount level, margin valorization, product mix, and long-term strategy.

Ready, set, action!
- ☐ Are all of your proposals sent to your customers maximizing value?
- ☐ Are your deals heavily discounted?
- ☐ Are you satisfied with your forecast accuracy?
- ☐ How can you update the compensation plan to make it a win-win sales/company?

CHAP 24: HUNT & HIRE TOP TALENT

Moneyball[61]

It is no secret that hiring salespeople can be a struggle, and that hiring the wrong person costs the company a lot. From the time spent on the recruitment process to recruitment agency fees, training expenses, and lost productivity, the costs can pile up quickly – without even considering the negative impact on team morale.

To identify key strategies, we will dive into the plot of Moneyball. Billy Beane develops tactics to recruit players and achieve results at the lowest possible expense.

With well-funded American startups opening offices on this side of the pond, there's even more pressure. Often, an executive team will be desperate enough to

---

[61] Photo by Brandon Mowinkel

raise the average salary only to recruit a talent that, yes, has credentials and might have been successful elsewhere but isn't a perfect fit.

Billy Beane: 'I can't compete against 120 million payrolls with 38 million dollars.'
Stephen Schott: 'We're not going to compete with these teams that have big budgets. We're going to work with the constraints that we have, and you're going to get out and do the best job that you can by recruiting new players. We're not going to pay 17 million dollars a year to players.'

How do you manage an efficient and cost-effective recruitment process, then? Knowing how talented salespeople make a decision is a start.

They base their decision on three main criteria:

--People--

Is the executive team inspiring? Is the company culture energizing? Is the hiring manager driven? Is he/she a coach? A possible mentor even?
Great employees are attracted by excellence. Some come as a pack: you hire a manager, and his/her old team follows; it works if and when the manager has done due diligence, accepting the challenges for what they are without turning a blind eye.

--Product--

A friend recently told me, 'I joined this company because they are smart, and they have 0% churn! I didn't even know that was possible.'

I didn't either! As a sales rep or leader, it is comforting to know that the product is not only reliable, but it is delivering actual value. Your trust is your reputation; your reputation is your success.

--Opportunity--

The package is one thing, but what the good recruiters use to seduce the great talent is more than just the opportunity to join the company. You may have a great package and never achieve your variable; you may have an average package and overachieve consistently.

Some salespeople see the opportunity, a life change: million-dollar commissions, stock options... and so on. Don't push a package. Push a great comp plan and possibly, great stock vesting.

Now that you know how they choose; act to attract them.

Billy Beane: 'I made one decision in my life based on money. And I swore I would never do it again.'

Think outside the box:
The best salespeople are naturally driven and highly coachable; they learn from their experience and show great resilience and adaptability. Last but not least, they learn fast. Recruit on these traits. Personality is everything. Take some risks in the profile you choose and teach them everything, coach them, and develop them. The Return on Time Invested here might be worth your extra mile.

Peter Brand: 'People are overlooked for a variety of biased reasons and perceived flaws. Age, appearance, personality.'

Have a plan:

Don't get seduced by the people with great numbers. Numbers can be faked. Interviews can be faked. Put them in situations: tell them to come with a presentation and give them 40 minutes to present it. If they've done their research; if they remain calm when you challenge them; if they ask questions and present themselves as a trusted advisor, give them the green card. Put your candidate *in situ* and use your best judge of characters by asking them to run unofficial interviews.

Billy Beane: 'This is the new direction for the Oakland A's. We are card counters at the Blackjack table, but we're going to turn the odds on the casino.'

Be human in your process. Inspire excellence. Many CEOs will have a LinkedIn post that says, 'Contact me, I'm hiring!' – but tend to push candidates back to recruiting agencies (best case) or never even consider an answer (worst case). Treat all of your candidates like potential customers; use social media and employee advocacy to promote why it is great to work at your company. Your best references and bait are your current successful employees.

Billy Beane: 'Then what the fuck are you talking about, man? If we try to play like the Yankees in here, we will lose to the Yankees out there.'

I have had the chance to work with amazing recruiters –not just agencies, but actual people. They make a difference with their tenacity in finding the right contact and qualifying them. Value their investment in understanding your value proposition and how to position it. They can make the great candidates excited to work with you and communicate between both parties to make amazing things happen. You should always free up the time and money to hire a headhunter.

Peter Brand: 'Your goal shouldn't be to buy players. Your goal should be to buy wins. In order to buy wins, you need to buy runs.'

Plot summary
- ☐ Great talents base their career decision on the people they join, the product they will sell and the opportunity.
- ☐ Put the candidate in situ to get a really good character perspective.
- ☐ Think outside the box to lure the candidates.

Ready, set, action!
- ☐ Do you have a strict recruiting process and are you satisfied with it?
- ☐ Do you ask the top candidates what would prevent them from joining your company?
- ☐ What are your key values? Cultural match is as important as skills and experience, make sure your candidates are in line with your company values?

CHAP 25: TOP ACHIEVER MANAGEMENT

Top Gun[62]

The Elite Navy Strike Fighter Tactics Instructor school opened in 1969. It is commonly known as the 'Top Gun' training program. To manage, train, develop, and retain Revenue Top Achievers, the risk-taking hot-shot elite of your organization, you may find inspiration in said program.

The top achievers blow your mind with ideas for pipeline generation. They have no fear of going after the biggest deals and have enough ambition to cover all teams. They are the people you cannot imagine doing without. Yet, they are the type of person whose self-confidence and borderline arrogance get under your skin.

---

[62] Photo Credit: Cibi Chakravarthi

Stinger: 'Don't screw around with me Maverick. You're a hell of an instinctive pilot. Maybe too good. I'd like to bust your butt, but I can't.'

Top Achievers win and own their titles. Often called 'Alpha' -I have unfortunately heard 'Diva' for females-, their peers consider them both admirable and frustrating.

Viper: 'In case some of you are wondering who the best is, they are up here on this plaque. Do you think your name will be on that plaque?'
Maverick: 'Yes, Sir.'
Viper: 'That's pretty arrogant, considering the company you're in.'
Maverick: 'Yes, Sir.'
Viper: 'I like that in a pilot.'

As a manager, assisting a Top Achiever in consistently overachieving requires skills and talent. How do you avoid falling into exasperating behaviors? How do you avoid micromanagement when you notice that they tend not to respect the rules to achieve? Or, on the opposite, how do you not fall into complete lack of management? If your Top Achievers break the rules to the eyes of all but in exchange bringing the largest deals of the year… or even the decade.

Goose: 'It's time for the big one.'
Iceman: 'You up for this one, Maverick?'
Maverick: 'Just a walk in the park, Kazansky.'

Often, because of their genius creative approach and numbers backing them up, the Top Achievers are quickly forgiven, even by the top management. Most of their peers close their eyes and accept that they don't fit in the lines, that they don't fill out the CRM as they should or that they have a special bond with legal and sales operations. As long as they are not toxic and people enjoy working with them, everything is fine. Until, one day, the balance is somehow disturbed. Your company's future is at risk because that one person stepped one too many times out of line.

Iceman: 'You're everyone's problem. That's because every time you go up in the air, you're unsafe. I don't like you because you're dangerous.'

So how do you manage a Top Achiever? Go back to the Maslow Pyramid and identify the basic sales requirements: money or/and recognition.

Slider: 'Remember, boys, no points for second place.'

If someone steps out of line, it should impact their commissions[63]. If a Top Achiever shares his/her knowledge and skills with others, applaud with recognition. Anyone in the company should be accountable for their actions, especially your Top Achievers.

---

[63] Refer to Chap 23: The art of the compensation plan

Stinger: 'Maverick, you just did an incredibly brave thing. (Pause) What you should have done was land your plane! You don't own that plane! The taxpayers do! Son, your ego is writing checks your body can't cash!'

The most intricate part is to retain and develop these talents. Challenging them by giving them tough customer accounts, bigger quotas to achieve, pushing them to the extreme is not a way of establishing a long-term relationship. On the opposite, it might make them leave. However, for some illogical reason, the leadership is pushing them to consistently bring more, relying on their revenue locomotive.

Instead, get to know what they want to do next in their career, what drives them. At the moment, their prime drive is money, and working tough accounts is what they like, or maybe, they may be interested in global account management, or hunting new logos, or specializing in a vertical sector. You can retain them by knowing what is important to them.

Have quarterly Skill/Will reviews. What do they want to achieve? What are their goals? And what are the skill gaps to get there? How can you help them develop and reach the next level of their career? What is their will? Are they getting bored? Demotivated? Are they starting to be toxic, or on the contrary are they going above and beyond for the team?

Stinger: 'They gave you your choice of duty, son. Anything, anywhere. Do you believe that shit? Where do you think you wanna go?'

Maverick: 'I thought of being an instructor, Sir.'
Stinger: 'Top Gun?'
Maverick:' Yes, Sir.'
Stinger: 'God help us.'

Plot summary
- ☐ Manage Top Achievers by understanding what drives them.
- ☐ Make it clear that they should not step out of line with consequences to their compensation plan.
- ☐ Have a quarterly review to analyze skills and gaps to write together a development plan and ensure retention.

Ready, set, action!
- ☐ Are you managing your sales team based on meritocracy?
- ☐ Are you making sure that Top Skills from each individual are shared across the team, recorded and documented?
- ☐ Have you ever been in the situation of having to let go of your top rep because of toxic behavior? How could you have prevented it?

CHAP 26: PROMOTE OR NOT PROMOTE

The Goonies[64]

Meritocracy is a common practice in leadership sales. If done properly, it creates a healthy competition and a sense of belonging. If it is not structured and planned carefully, it can become a disastrous booby trap for promotion failures and toxic behavior.

Promoting a young and avid sales representative without giving him/her the proper time to develop his/her skills through experience is a mistake any founder can make. - It does not mean however that one should remain in the same role for years either-

Chunk: 'You guys, I'm hungry. I know when my stomach growls there's trouble.'

---

[64] Photo by Zoltan Tasi

A young, inexperienced, and recently promoted manager can quickly feel under pressure, leading to excessive stress, micromanagement, toxic behavior, and failure.

Mikey: 'We had our hands on the future, but we blew it to save our own lives... Sorry.'

A manager is not born. It is made.

Experience is not the only criteria when promoting someone from individual contributor to manager. With all promotions, you should proceed with caution, patience, and reflection. Your top sales representative is your cash cow, make sure they understand the positive and negative consequences of moving to a new role.

A manager rarely overachieves and hits the commission targets as a top sales representative can. The slight increase of 'on target' earnings (OTE) will never compete with a great sales record.
Ask them bluntly: 'Are you ok to take a pay cut?'

Stef: 'This is ridiculous. It's crazy. I feel like I'm babysitting, except I'm not getting paid.'

Asking the right questions will lead you to comprehend your superstar's true motivation to become a sales manager. Ego should never be a reason. Answers such as 'I need to progress in my career' or 'It is the next natural step' should sound the alarm bell. You are going down the wrong route, and so are they. However, if the answers are 'growing at a personal level' or 'willingness to give back and develop others' then, you might be onto something good. These answers are the perfect starters to move the conversation to a deeper level and possibly start writing a development plan.

The next important question that you must ask is: 'If I promote you, who will be your backup?' As a rule of thumb, any successful leader has to be thinking about their replacement to ensure their team and department security and growth.

This will give you insights into how seriously your top sales representative has been considering the impact of stepping into a leadership position. You want someone who demonstrates that they can think strategically. Someone who is a team player and thinks of the team's future first (right answer) rather than a person who is thinking solely about his or her advancement (wrong answer).

Mikey: 'Don't you guys see? Don't you realize? He was a pro. He never made it this far. Look how far we've come. We've got a chance.'

Another thing to consider is that the transition to learn something new takes time. For people who were at the top of their game, it might be annoying not to excel right away in their new role. Make sure to plan the transition with a proper development plan and clear warning on the challenging times ahead. Stepping into management is like stepping into parenthood: it requires patience, the courage to let your people fail and learn, and more importantly, the ability to be caring and supportive without overstepping.

Mama Fratelli: 'Kids suck.'

Under the pressure of a global team quota, your new manager will probably forget their leader role and responsibilities to act as individual contributor.

This should be an immediate warning: a leader should always be there to support the team. Yet, never should he/she act on one of his/her team members' behalf. This type of attitude should be called out immediately to let your new leader develop into a true leader, no matter the pressure of the numbers.

You can pick up such attitudes from the smallest actions, such as taking a call to close a deal on the rep's behalf. Educate, teach, use psychology. Put your manager back in the sales rep's seat. How would they have felt if someone else had done it to them?

Insider tip, they may come up with excuses such as:

- I was the sales rep on this account, the customer is used to talking to me.
- My sales rep was on vacation.
- The prospect will only move forward if they talk to me.

Don't be fooled. Act on it, refocus them where they should be in their new leadership role.

Elgin Perkins: 'Is your mommy here?'
Brandon Walsh: 'No, sir. Actually, she's out at the market buying Pampers for all us kids.'

Does it mean you should not promote your best people? Absolutely not. Everyone deserves their own time to grow into a challenging position. Remember that the overachievers do not make the best managers and vice versa.

First, assess the situation with a skill/will program. This will combine an evaluation of the capabilities required to successfully achieve in their role (skills) and evaluate their motivation towards the positive impact they can bring (will).

Organize a formal review with the objective of writing a development plan. This interview should cover questions such as:

☐ How do they rate themselves from one to four in their current role (capability to generate new opportunities, the capability to execute on an account plan, the capability to access the executives at prospects…)?

☐ Are they consciously competent or unconsciously competent?

- Do you believe they can teach, coach, and transmit their skills to others, or do they believe it is inherent to their own character?

- How satisfied are they with their current role?

- Are they eager to move to another role, and if so, which?

Build a path to their next role. Keep your best people, train them, develop them.

Mikey: 'Don't you realize? The next time you see the sky, it'll be over another town. The next time you take a test, it'll be in some other school. Our parents, they want the best of stuff for us. But right now, they got to do what's right for them because it's their time. Their time! Up there! Down here, it's our time. It's our time down here.'

There might be times when despite your efforts of teaching, coaching, providing the right tools and language, it does not translate well into actions. This is unfortunately the sign your newly promoted representative was not ready for the task.

Irene Walsh: 'Pants and shirts go in the… oh, forget about it. Just throw everything into cardboard boxes. Clark, can you really translate all that?'
Mouth: 'For sure, Mrs. Walsh. (In Spanish) The marijuana goes in the top drawer. The cocaine and speed go in the second drawer. And the heroin goes in the bottom drawer. Always separate the drugs.'

Some of the best career examples I have witnessed and who later became VP of Sales/Chief Revenue Officer were promoted by a Mentor who stayed by their side throughout their transition. From Sales to Manager, Manager to Director, Director to VP and so on. You are not born a leader; you are made one by another.

It is not the place of a CEO to promote a sales representative to a leadership position if he cannot provide the mentoring needed for them to learn how to teach, coach, develop, recruit and forecast.

A mentor will prepare his mentee to delegate, trust, build, recruit, and, more importantly, take assertive decisions. A mentor will back up his/her mentee in all their decisions because they remember they once were in these shoes; they once made mistakes and were covered.

Forgive and forget, train, and develop again.

Andy: 'I hit the wrong note. I'm not Liberace, you know!'

Plot summary
- ☐ Understand why you are promoting your top achiever.
- ☐ Ensure your new manager does not fall back into the individual contributor role under pressure.
- ☐ Create a skill/will program and development plan.
- ☐ Assign a mentor: to be successful in a new challenging role, your new manager will require guidance and support.

Ready, set, action!
- ☐ Are you promoting your top sales representative to avoid hiring an expensive manager externally?
- ☐ Do you have a plan to make the transition successful? Are you aligned with the reasons for the promotion and the results expected?

CHAP 27: OBJECTIONS AND REJECTIONS

Love Actually[65]

Whether you are looking for investments, securing new customers, or adding top talents, objections, and rejections are the entrepreneur's daily bread. Receiving objections is never a pleasant moment. However, with practice and preparation, it can become easier to handle and be made less painful.

Prepare for objections

---

[65] Photo credit Clem-onojeghuo

No one else better than you know your weaknesses and their origins. No one else better than you know how you address these weaknesses. List them all, match them with a plan to overcome with your current strengths. Make an exhaustive list; do not overlook any difficult ones. Be resilient.

Colin: 'No, I'm wise. Stateside I am Prince William without the weird family.'

Provoke them, get them in the open

Some of your interlocutors will not dare to tell you what they really think, what is bothering them. If you do not provoke the conversation, you cannot address the objections. A talent you have been hunting might wish to sign with a larger company such as Google or Amazon because of the benefits and security. A customer would rather sign with your competitor because they did not understand your long-term vision. Hoping the deal will go through is not enough.

Mia: 'I'll be hanging around the mistletoe, hoping to be kissed.'
You can control objections. Ask the tough questions, not for your interlocutor, but yourself. The added benefit is that you give them confidence that you can handle anything by putting yourself at risk in the open.

These questions will work with any relationship, whether you are trying to close an investment, get talent to sign their contract, or a customer to engage with you.

- ☐ What would prevent you from signing with us?

- ☐ Is there anything that is worrying you in our long-term partnership?

- ☐ Are there any elements of concern you would like to address?

An objection is a way of saying 'No' to something. The sooner you address the issue, the better chances you have to turn the odds in your favor. In weddings, the question 'Does anyone object to this union?' is always offered before concluding the agreement. Why not apply this symbolic common sense to business?

Daniel: 'Tell her that you love her. You've got nothing to lose, and you'll always regret it if you don't.'

Be ready to handle them.

How you react under pressure and how calm you remain under attack is 90% of the objection handling. Do not try under any circumstances to justify yourself. Instead, remain empathetic, attentive, and non-judgmental.

The first step to objection handling is to listen and let your interlocutor express its concerns. Take notes, ask additional questions as you would when uncovering a problem, you can solve. Become a friendly, caring detective to find the objection's root cause: the origin of the fear. Here your utmost natural art of connection is required to avoid the feeling of an aggressive interrogation room!

Once you've uncovered the cradle of the objection: reformulate. Make sure you did not interpret what your investor, or talent, or prospect is saying. When under pressure, we tend to understand certain words differently or even make our interpretations based on past experiences or scenarios we've made up in our head.

Natalie: "Thank you, sir. I did have an awful premonition that I was gonna fuck up on the first day. Oh, piss it!"

Providing a detailed summary to your interlocutor builds up even more trust. You've listened, you've understood, and you are making sure that your understanding is correct.

Last but not least, provide a response that you have worked on in the preparation phase. Are investors challenging your forecast accuracy?

You may not have fixed the issue, though you know about it and have a plan to fix it, present it. Reassure, build trust and confidence. Does a talent feel that there is too much risk joining a startup? Maybe it was not a personality fit, acknowledge their fear of risk, and ask them what motivated them to interview with a startup in the first place. Is a prospect not clear on your roadmap? Understand where you lost them and offer a detailed workshop to provide them with your vision.

Jamie, speaking broken Portuguese: 'Sometimes, things are so transparency. They don't need evidential proof.'

Better known than continue blindly.

There will be objections that you will not be able to handle, and rejections will endure. Going through these unpleasant moments is the main reason why anyone avoids asking the tough questions. It is ok.

Karen: 'Would you stay, knowing life would always be a little bit worse? Or would you cut and run?'

Knowing early that a candidate will not sign with you allows you to go on the hunt for another candidate sooner than later. It is the same for customers. Some will not be ready to move forward.

It is better to generate a sales pipeline early on, knowing that you will not close the deal rather than maintain a fake pipeline and announce a non-accurate forecast to your executives and investors at the last minute of the quarter.

Knowing first that rejection is bound to happen empowers you to bounce back even though your company and self-ego might still feel a bit bruised.

Daniel: 'Well, we need Kate, and we need Leo, and we need them now.'

The life of an entrepreneur is full of ups and downs. There will be days when you feel like the King/Queen of the world and others when you wonder why you even started.

Keep the why always close to your heart, passion, drive, and will, and remember that, even if you fail, it's only part of the learning process.

> *'But for now, let me say,*
> *without hope or agenda,*
> *just because it's Christmas*
> *(and at Christmas, you tell the truth)*
> *to me, you are perfect'*
> *– Mark, Love Actually*

Plot summary
- Prepare for objections, get them in the open, handle them.
- It is better to know early to put a remediation plan in motion.
- Failing and rejection will happen, it is part of the process, the sooner you accept the more resilient you will become.

Ready, set, action!
- Are you wearing the pink glasses or listing all the things that can go wrong?
- Can you take a moment to sit down with your team and write all potential objections? Are they justified? How can you come around them?
- What is your set of strengths?

UNTIL THE SEQUEL

The Art of War by Sun Tzu
Good To Great by Jim Collins
Behind the Cloud by Marc Benioff
The Challenger Sale: Taking Control of the Customer Conversation by Matthew Dixon and Brent Adamson
The Hard Thing About Hard Things by Ben Horowitz
Crossing the Chasm (3rd edition) by Geoffrey A. Moore
Let My People Go Surfing: The Education of a Reluctant Businessman--Including 10 More Years of Business Unusual by Yvon Chouinard
MEDDICC: The ultimate guide to staying one step ahead in the complex sale by Mr Andy Whyte
The Sandler Rules: 49 Timeless Selling Principles…and How to Apply Them by David Mattson and Sandler Training
Negotiating with Giants: Get What You Want Against the Odds Negotiating with Giants by Peter Johnston
First, Break All the Rules: What the World's Greatest Managers Do Differently Hardcover by Marcus Buckingham

THANK YOU SPEECH

'Films and life are like clay, waiting for us to mold it. And when you trust your own insides and that becomes achievement, it's a kind of a principal that seems to me that works with everyone,'

Shirley MacLaine
Best Actress for "Terms of Endearment" in 1984

I would like to express my utmost gratitude to the people who have been part of this journey.

My loving and supporting husband, Romain Franczia, the first reader of everything I write.

Amirhossein Malekzadeh, Ekaterina Walter for writing a wonderful foreword.

The absolute best sparring partner and editor one could dream of: David Johnson (Maddyness), also author of the back cover quote.

The gang of women who empower women: Caroline Krancenblum, Carine Guillaume, Barbara Rousseau, Anne Sophie Cardon, Pauline Clairet, Shibani Baksi, Joana Pais, Sabrina Lefevre, Florence de Vesvrotte, Judith Tripard, Ekaterina Walter, Wendy Wilson Howard, Olga Katzelnik.

A network of people who offered advice, coaching and mentoring along my professional path and without whom this content would not even exist:

The BMC gang for a proper introduction to MEDDIC and what true execution means: José Martins, Jeremy Bellaiche, Karim Larbi, Thibaud Ceyrolle, Pascal Dallioux, Alexandre Pierrin Neron, Stephane Chantalou, Paul Cant, Cedric Pech, Jeremy Duggan, Jason Andrew.

The Sprinklr gang for a proper introduction to the startup life and absolute passion toward one common goal - BELIEVEITIS- (Dick Dunkel, Ragy Thomas, Sebastien Boitelle, Jerome Beauguitte, Aref Jdey, Nicolas Spie, Elisabeth B Closmore, Hélène Quevreux, Andrea Rabiant, Matthew Birbeck, Vesna Cosich, Julien Leblanc, Celia Goletto, Charlotte Lesage, Raphael Guerard).

The Datadog gang for an experience I will never forget: Sebastien Boitelle, Oceane Fievet, Amirhossein Malekzadeh, Renaud Boutet, Philippe Ramanantsoa, Pierre Guceski, Pejman Tabassomi.

The best champions I've had the chance to work with: Jean-Michel Garcia, Stephan Garandet, Jean Denis Mariani, Michael Aidan, Francis Manzac.

The Uppercut First family and incredible advisors: Romain Vidal, Andy Whyte, Romaric Philogène, Morgan Perry, Jerome Joaug, David Keribin, Adam Kurkiewicz, Antoine Leprince. Veronica Prato Peraza (art director)

All clients, prospects, accelerators and VCs I have the chance to work with and anyone who attended the office hours.

Last but not least, my parents and grandparents for teaching me how to read and write from the earliest day and my little monkeys that are not so little anymore: Romeo & Theodore to whom this book is dedicated.

'And I know we're forgetting somebody.' Ben Affleck
'Whoever we forgot we love you! We love you!' Matt Damon

Ben Affleck and Matt Damon Oscars
Acceptance speech of Good Will Hunting

ABOUT THE AUTHOR

Caroline Franczia (Sprinklr, Datadog) is a seasoned sales expert. After starting her career with large tech companies (Computer Associates, Oracle, BMC Software), she spent four years in the Silicon Valley, soaking in Startup culture. A regular columnist for Maddyness UK and founder of Uppercut First, she's become, in 2020, the European tech Startups CEO's whisperer through hundreds of office hours.[66]

---

[66] Photo Credit Aurore Vinot www.aurorevinot.com

Printed in Great Britain
by Amazon